CIGAR FAMILY

A 100 YEAR JOURNEY
IN THE CIGAR INDUSTRY

Stanford J. Newman with James V. Miller

Introduction by Marvin R. Shanken

CUSTOM PUBLISHING

CIP Data is available
Printed in the United States of America
10 9 8 7 6 5 4 3 2 1

ISBN: 0–8281–1339–4

To the memory of my mother and father,

to my loving wife, children, and grandchildren,

and to the Carlos Fuente family.

TO Max,

Best wishes to
a good friend.

5/17/00

Acknowledgements

I first want to thank my sons, Eric and Bobby, whose support and enthusiasm for this project never wavered. I could not have completed my book without them.

I also want to thank my collaborator, James Miller, who shaped my many reminiscences into a coherent narrative. Thanks also go to researcher and historian Glen Westfall, and to the publishing team at Forbes Inc.

Finally, my deepest gratitude to the special friends and mentors who helped me make all my smoke dreams come true: the Angel and Karl Cuesta family, the Carlos Fuente family, the Angel Oliva family, Marvin R. Shanken, Anton van Beck, Lee Bentley, and Max Hollingsworth.

Contents

NTRODUCTION

Cigars have been a life-long passion for me. I've smoked for nearly thirty years. But it was not until 1992 that I fulfilled my own dream of publishing a cigar magazine. After the launch of *Cigar Aficionado*, it didn't take long for me to discover that the world of cigars was filled with people just like me—people who love cigars. But in so many cases, they are even luckier. They belong to families that have lived cigars not just for a few years, but for generations. One of those families is the Newmans: Stanford, and his sons Bobby and Eric. *Cigar Family* is their story of 100 years in the cigar industry.

The Newmans epitomize all that is great about the family nature of the cigar business. Stanford Newman's father, J.C. Newman, started the dream, and now his grandchildren are leading the company into the twenty-first century. Even J.C.'s great-grandchildren are already being groomed for the family business. From the Newmans' roots in Cleveland, they have built a thriving business today that is spreading their Cuesta-Rey and Diamond Crown brands all over the world. It is a success story based on the values of integrity and hard work, and most of all, family.

Cigar Family is about the realization of an American Dream. It's about dedication to a purpose, and perseverance even during the 1970s and 1980s when cigar sales were nearly snuffed out altogether. The Newmans not only survived this dark period, but they've built on their dreams, and created a bright future for generations to come.

Marvin R. Shanken
Editor & Publisher
Cigar Aficionado

THE VALUE OF A DOLLAR

I could not have been more than five years old when I visited my father's cigar factory for the first time. I will never forget the pungent smell of tobacco that permeated every corner of the factory and clung to my skin and clothes; the moist, leathery texture of the tobacco leaves between my fingers; the unintelligible sound of hundreds of women chattering away in Hungarian as they rolled cigars by hand, their voices echoing across the immense factory floor. These strange new sights and sounds and smells would soon become second nature to me.

I was born on June 12, 1916, in Cleveland, Ohio, and grew up immersed in the history and traditions of the cigar industry. My father was a self-made man who came to America from his native Hungary in 1888 at the age of thirteen with almost nothing to his name, speaking not a word of English. He went on to build one of the most successful cigar companies in Cleveland before I was even born. He had witnessed the erratic growth of the American cigar industry firsthand, fighting his way to the top from the bottom of the trenches.

My father's first two children were girls, a fact that sorely disappointed him. He longed for a boy whom he could groom as his successor in the family cigar business. The story goes that while my mother was pregnant with me, my father became seriously ill. He was so happy when I came along as his first-born son that he immediately recovered from his prolonged illness and never suffered another sick day in his life.

My father's full name was Julius Caesar Newman. I cannot imagine anything more appropriate. He actually didn't have a middle name until he registered to vote in the United States. A clerk told him that a middle name was required, and suggested the example of

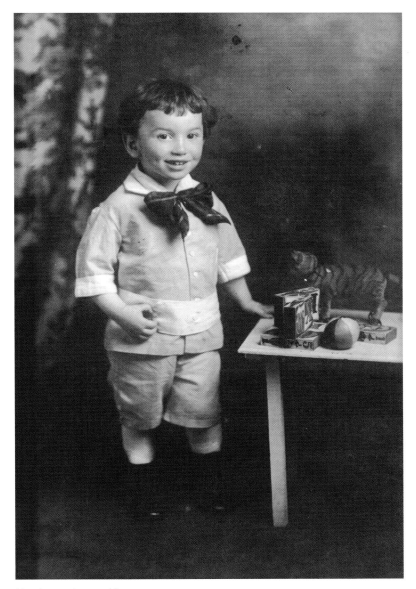

Here I am, at the age of four

another Julius: the most famous conqueror in history. My father liked the sound of that, took the middle name of Caesar, and forever after went by his new initials: J.C.

J.C. had something in common with another of the world's great conquerors. At five foot three, he was short enough to earn comparisons to Napoleon. Some people also referred to him as Little Caesar after the diminutive gangster played by Edward G. Robinson in the classic 1930 gangster film, but not to his face.

Because of my father's Napoleonic complex, everything around him had to be big. He owned the biggest cigar factory in town, was chauffeured in a gigantic Cadillac limousine, and lived in a huge house in East Cleveland, Ohio, decorated with ornate marble sculptures

J.C. Newman

and expensive oil paintings. It almost felt like a museum. With twelve rooms, three garages, and a grand ballroom on the third floor, there was plenty of room for my brother and sisters and me to run around.

I did many unorthodox things in our ballroom during my childhood. It was an excellent place to play hockey. I used to remove the heels from my father's shoes and use them as pucks. I built a boxing ring and held boxing matches. I even turned the ballroom into a makeshift movie theatre and charged the neighborhood kids two cents each to watch movies.

My father was the shortest person in our household, but he had the biggest ego. J.C. was an autocrat who expected his children to follow orders. He had an opinion on everything, and his opinion was always final. He used to come to dinner with a cane and pound the table for silence when anyone questioned his authority.

Of the four children in our household, two of them—my sister Elaine and my brother Millard—inherited my father's personality. Elaine was a wild tiger and Millard was a maverick. Both of them did just as they pleased. Naturally, this led to a great many disagreements

CIGAR FAMILY

Gladys with her first-born, Helen

The Newman family (clockwise):
Gladys, Elaine, J.C., Helen, me, and Millard (1921)

with our father. Millard would lock himself in his bedroom to escape our father's lectures. Millard had a great sense of humor and we got along pretty well. He was also a talented musician who could play almost any instrument. The violin was his specialty. My other sister, Helen, had a friendly disposition, and was very intelligent.

Compared to my brother and sisters, I was sensitive and shy. I suppose I was compensating for their excess of personality. I was the most levelheaded, least high-strung person in the house, with the possible exception of my mother, Gladys, who could not have been more of a contrast to my father. She was refined, gentle and kind. He raised his voice at the slightest provocation. She had

Gladys Newman and her children

attended finishing school. He had almost no formal education. Somehow, their personalities worked together. One thing they had in common was that they both spoke German and often used it to tell each other things they didn't want their children to understand.

Of all of us in that huge house in East Cleveland, my mother was the one who knew just how to get along with J.C. She would listen to him lay down the law, politely nod her head in agreement, and then go out and do her own thing. She was home for my father every evening, but the daytime was hers to live her own life. She was very active socially and supported many charities, especially children's causes. Not only did she teach child psychology and serve as chairman of Cleveland's Federation of Child Study for eight years, she was also a talented writer and a lifelong member of Pen Women of America.

When I was fourteen years old, my mother decided to run as a candidate for the school board. I drove her around town while she was campaigning. (I'll explain later how I came to be driving a car at the age of fourteen.) My mother knew nothing about politics—she thought she could just run for the office and win. She lost. She was more successful on the home front, where I sometimes enlisted her as an ally in my frequent battles with my father.

J.C. Newman spent lavishly on all the trappings of a successful businessman's lifestyle, but when it came to his children, he was frugal to a fault. Money for toys—or hockey pucks— was hard to come by. I remember playing with my father's shoes when I was five years old, tying several pairs together by the laces and pretending they were a train.

My father's chief concern in raising his children, which he drilled into us again and again, was to teach us the value of a dollar. Making money was very important to him, although not as an end in itself. He believed that success was measured by material possessions. Money allowed you to acquire the things society associates with success.

Unfortunately, learning the value of a dollar left little time for extracurricular activities. During the summers of my youth, while my friends were outdoors playing sports or attending summer camp, I was usually indoors working. The irony was that my father actually had a great fondness for the outdoors. He had grown up with the Hungarian countryside as his backyard. He loved to exercise and did so every morning of his life. When I was a teenager, we took long walks together every evening after dinner. As we walked the ten blocks to our neighborhood drug store, he would talk to me about growing up in Hungary and how proud he was to be living the American Dream.

GLADYS R. NEWMAN

(Mrs. J. C.)

INDEPENDENT CANDIDATE

FOR

SCHOOL BOARD

EAST CLEVELAND

Mrs. Newman has been a resident of East Cleveland for over 13 years. She is a mother of four children, two of whom have gone through East Cleveland Schools and graduated from Shaw High, and two who are at present attending high school.

Gladys Newman, young wife, mother and philanthropist, runs for East Cleveland School Board

Have you ever asked yourself the question? Why is it that our salaries and incomes are reduced everywhere, and yet taxes are as high as during the war?

STOP AND THINK!

It's Politics

If I am elected, I pledge to work for a reduction in Taxes and to keep politics out of schools.

I am not affiliated with any political organization and will not be indebted to any politician.

Mrs. Newman was chairman for 8 years of Chapter 44 of the Federation of Child Study of Cleveland, and is now a member of Adult Education of Cleveland College.

GLADYS R. NEWMAN

(Mrs. J. C.)

INDEPENDENT CANDIDATE

(NON-PARTISAN TICKET)

FOR SCHOOL BOARD

EAST CLEVELAND

7◁▷1

THIS MEANS

IN YOUR POCKETS

READ THIS PAMPHLET

He liked searching for four-leaf clovers as we walked. You could find them pressed into the pages of almost every book he owned. Despite my father's imperious personality, he was at heart an optimist who believed everything was possible if you worked hard enough. He taught me never to give up, that there was always a way out of any bad situation. I made an effort to listen to my father, although it wasn't always easy. We were very close; we just didn't always get along.

In 1924 I tried to emulate him by becoming a young entrepreneur, selling lemonade for three cents a glass at a small stand in front of our house. I was eight years old. We were on a main street in East Cleveland and many people stopped by for a cold glass of lemonade in the hot summertime. My first business was a success.

I grew up in that notorious decade known as the Roaring Twenties. It was an exciting time for new inventions. Radio was the most popular new technology of the day. I bought my first radio when I was ten years old—a Crystal Set that I assembled myself—and listened to "Amos and Andy" every week. Our family also owned a Victrola, the best phonograph there was. It really was a piece of furniture. My sister, Elaine, the wild one, would wind it up, put on the latest jazz record, and dance so hard the turntable jiggled.

These were also the days of Prohibition, when drinking alcohol was outlawed by the federal government for nearly fourteen years. Our family knew all the bootleggers in Cleveland. In 1930 at the age of fourteen, I became a bootlegger myself, although only for a single night.

In 1930 my sister, Helen, got married. She was the more agreeable of my two sisters and I wanted to do something special for her wedding. Being in the cigar business during Prohibition had its advantages. My father had obtained a federal permit to legally purchase alcohol for manufacturing purposes. He would mix a solution of wine, raw alcohol, and molasses, which he used as a catalyst to ferment tobacco and improve its taste and burning qualities.

Six months before Helen's wedding, and unbeknownst to my father, I convinced our factory superintendent to slip me a little pure alcohol on the sly—"for a good cause," I assured him. The problem of how to turn it into something drinkable was solved by a fellow who sold all sorts of paraphernalia to bootleggers. Conveniently, his establishment was located next door to my father's factory. From him I purchased some rye whiskey extract and a small charcoal-lined barrel. I mixed the rye extract with pure alcohol and poured the mixture into the barrel. I then hid the barrel in a small room off the ballroom on the third floor and let the mixture ferment for six months.

When guests entered the ballroom for my sister's wedding reception, they were delighted to find a keg of rye whiskey set up at the bar. It was the hit of the party and almost everyone got drunk. Just when the fun was really getting started, at ten o'clock on the dot, my father suddenly stood up and announced to the assembled guests, "Goodnight, folks!" and, without further ado, strode off to bed. My mother was furious with him, but it was his lifelong habit to go to bed at 10 p.m., no matter what was going on, even with a house full of company.

Another way I got my kicks in the Roaring Twenties was by hot-wiring my father's Model T Ford. I was twelve years old and itching to drive a car. I didn't know how to drive, but I thought: Let's see if I can get it started, then I'll worry about how to drive it.

I stuck a knife in the ignition and wiggled it around for what seemed an eternity. Just when I was ready to give up—music to my ears—the engine sprang to life! Now that I had figured out how to start the car, I took it out for a test drive. It was one thing to watch my parents drive. It was something else entirely to do it myself, but I got the hang of it soon enough. I had a grand time cruising down the avenues of East Cleveland—a twelve-year-old kid behind the wheel of a shiny black Model T.

My newfound driving skills turned out to be a big help to my mother. She had her own car that she drove to luncheons and charity events practically every day. The problem was that she never learned how to back up. Every night after she brought her car home, I turned it around and backed it up into the garage for her so that she could get out the next day. By the time I turned sixteen and was issued my license, I was a seasoned driver. In those days, you just applied for a license and they gave it to you, no test required. To this day, I have never taken a driving test.

I also taught my brother, Millard, how to drive. Thus began his life-long fascination with automobiles. He bought his first used car at sixteen and from then on he was always underneath a hood, taking a motor out of one car and putting it into another. He almost always had grime under his fingernails. On Saturday nights, he would come in from the garage and wash his hands to go out on a date, but otherwise, he was always under the hood.

Like my brother, I was mechanically inclined, and I loved to make things out of wood. When I was eight years old, I set up a workshop in our basement equipped entirely from the Sears Roebuck catalogue. I ordered all the necessary tools and built footstools, chairs, and many other things. My mechanical skills came in handy in junior high school when my German teacher asked me to run the noon movies.

In those days, movie projectors used arc lights with charcoal lighters. You generated electricity by striking two pieces of charcoal together. It was like lighting a small fire. I ran two reels every day at noon for several years. When the school administration deemed a movie title too risqué for the students—*Ladies' Morals* is one I remember—they asked me to splice out the title, splice in something more acceptable, and we showed it anyway.

The twenties came roaring to a close when the stock market crashed at the end of October 1929, ushering in the Great Depression. It was a terrible time for everyone. People were jumping out of windows and killing themselves because they lost so much money. It was almost comical. A clerk with a very twisted sense of humor at the Hotel Pierre, then one of the tallest hotels in New York City, used to ask guests checking in at the time of the Stock Market Crash, "Will your room be for sleeping or jumping? If for jumping, I can put you on a higher floor."

When President Roosevelt declared a banking holiday in 1933 as part of his National Recovery Act, all the banks closed for ninety days. Unless you were there, it is impossible to imagine what it was like. You couldn't write a check. There was simply no money. County governments issued IOUs called scrip on the anticipation of income from real estate taxes, and almost everyone paid for things using half scrip and half cash.

One of my father's greatest lessons was that you had to be willing to expand your business during the bad times and conserve money during the good times. The Great Depression gave him the opportunity to put his philosophy to the test.

True to his word, my father invested as much in his business as he could during these bad times and managed to do surprisingly well. He kept his factory going at full capacity, operating two shifts throughout 1933, one of the worst years of the Depression, when a company as formidable as General Motors closed their Cleveland body plant for the entire year.

Gladys Newman at 22

During the Depression, my mother took it upon herself to support a poor family on the outskirts of Cleveland, using a portion of the weekly allowance my father gave her to provide them with food and clothing. She did this entirely behind his back. If he had found out about it, I'm sure he would have objected. My father felt his primary obligation was to his own family.

Although we never suffered like most people during the Depression, money was still tight. I showed I was truly my father's son by trying to save as much of it as I could. This required a certain amount of creativity.

During high school, my father gave me an allowance of a dollar a week to spend on lunch. At my school we had a choice of two lunch periods, starting at either eleven or twelve o'clock. I always chose the early lunch period, knowing I would be less hungry earlier in the day and spend less money on food. I felt I accomplished a lot if I spent eleven cents instead of sixteen. Sometimes my appetite got the better of me. When I was really hungry I would take a pickle and drop it in my soup while going through the cafeteria line. Not seeing the hidden pickle, the cashier charged me only for the soup. Desperate times called for desperate measures.

I graduated from Shaw High School in East Cleveland in 1934. There was never any question whether I would go on to college. My father believed in education. While I was growing up, he often took correspondence courses or attended seminars. He was especially interested in public speaking and would pace around the house all night practicing speeches while my brother and sisters and I were trying to study. We finally had to tell him to keep quiet or we would never graduate.

I had my heart set on attending the Wharton School of Finance at the University of Pennsylvania, which had a great reputation for business. It would have been quite a coup for me to attend this prestigious institution. Its distance from Cleveland would also provide the perfect getaway from my father. I thought my grades were good enough to gain entrance to Wharton, but my father prevailed upon me to study closer to home, where tuition would be less expensive and he could keep an eye on me. He believed the best learning took place in the home and insisted he could teach me more if I stayed under his wing.

Reluctantly, I enrolled at Western Reserve University in Cleveland, which later became Case Western Reserve. I majored in economics, the closest thing they had to business. Tuition was $150 a semester, considerably less than the Wharton School, but still a great deal during the Depression.

My first year was devoted mostly to my studies. I had labs in the afternoon, which left little time for work. My chemistry teacher inadvertently taught me the importance of good communication. He had the annoying habit of covering the chalkboard with symbols at incredible speed. He would pause for two seconds, ask "You got it?" and, without waiting for an answer, immediately erase everything he had just put up and begin filling the board all over again. I could only copy about half of it. Years later in our cigar factory, I was always careful to post notices for weeks at a time so everyone had time to read what management had to say.

I completed my freshman year of college in 1935. I was ready to go to work for the summer. I was so anxious to earn some money. There wasn't anybody in school who didn't supplement his studies with a job on the side. When my father's salesman for downtown Cleveland resigned, I saw my opportunity. I immediately arranged for a meeting with my father and his business partner, Grover Mendelsohn. I didn't waste any time.

"I'd like to be the downtown salesman," I said.

They had their reservations. Here I was, an eighteen-year-old college kid, asking for a position of considerable responsibility. But I was prepared to make my case. During high school I had spent my summer vacations working in the factory and learned a great deal about tobacco and the manufacturing process. I could even make my own cigars by hand.

"I admit I don't have any sales experience, but I grew up in this business and I know about cigars," I said. "I can use the sedan delivery truck we have parked at home. The company's not using it now anyway."

They were open to the idea, so I pressed on. I had one condition for taking the job. It was the key to achieving my financial independence. I was prepared to refuse the job if they didn't accept this one condition.

"I don't want a salary. Just pay me a ten percent sales commission and I'll cover all my own expenses."

You could have heard a pin drop in that room. Ten percent was a generous commission by any standards. For a college student with little or no sales experience, it was unheard of. They asked me to settle for less. They said they would increase my commission after I proved myself. I said no. It was ten percent or nothing. After a lot of arm twisting, they agreed to give me a chance. Thus began my career in the cigar industry.

Cleveland's new downtown salesman

I was pretty green when I first started making sales calls. It was hard for me because I was so shy. My first day at work I called on thirty people and didn't sell a single cigar. That night I thought it over and realized my problem: I was offering only one brand, asking my customers, "Would you like to buy some cigars?" A new strategy was called for. The next day, I went out with three different brands of cigars, asking a different question: "Which one would you like?" I sold ten individual boxes that day. I had learned my first important lesson in business: Customers like to have choices.

One of my routine duties as a salesman was to decorate, or "trim" as it was called, my customers' storefront window displays. As I made my rounds through downtown Cleveland, I trimmed each window with multi-colored crepe paper and posters to highlight an assortment of empty cigar boxes. My displays with cardboard dancing girls always caught people's attention. As part of the job, it was an expected courtesy that I wash each retailer's windows inside and out. I learned two things from the experience: first, the importance of presentation; second, that no job is beneath a good salesman who wants to earn his customer's good will.

During my first summer as a cigar salesman, I also learned it is not enough to *tell* someone about your cigar. You have to get him to *try* it. My technique was simple. As I visited one cigar store after another situated along the wide avenues and arcades of downtown Cleveland, I would walk up to a retailer, pull out a cigar, stick it in his mouth, and light it for him.

"Isn't that the best cigar you ever smoked?" I asked encouragingly.

On a good day, he would say, "It sure is, kid," and there was my sale. Sometimes, I would give another retailer the same cigar and get a very different reaction: "I'd say it's the worst I ever smoked! Get lost!"

It was frustrating to discover that our cigars did not appeal to everyone, but there was nothing I could do about it because I did not smoke them myself. Being of a fairly conservative nature, I never smoked cigars as a young man. And I couldn't make recommendations to our master tobacco blender on how to improve our cigars unless I knew how they tasted. But I was not ready to make that level of commitment to the cigar business just yet. I didn't begin to smoke cigars until the end of World War II.

As I began my sophomore year at Western Reserve in 1935, I arranged to take classes in the mornings so that I could work in the afternoons and study in the evenings. Between school and work, there wasn't much time left over for fun. Fraternity life was my salvation. In those days, if you were not a member of a fraternity, you did not have a social life. If I hadn't joined a fraternity, college would have been nothing more than overgrown high school.

I pledged Zeta Beta Tau. During Hell Week, the toilet paper was removed from all the bathrooms in the fraternity house and everyone had to come to me when they needed to use the bathroom. My job as "Keeper of the Toilet Paper" was to wear a roll around my neck and dispense it to all the other pledges, recording how many sheets I gave to each person. At the end of the week, I had to submit a report on my findings.

Another type of hazing that took place during my initiation occurred when another pledge and I were taken out in the middle of the night, driven fifteen miles from Cleveland, and left stranded on an isolated country road in the middle of winter. We were expected to find our way back to Cleveland with no money and were searched carefully to make sure we weren't carrying any cash.

I knew it was coming, however, and outsmarted my future fraternity brothers. The night before, I had removed the heel of my shoe and put a twenty-dollar bill under it before nailing the heel back on. My fellow pledge and I simply walked to the nearest farmhouse and called a taxicab to take us back to the center of town. I had deposited another $20 with a cashier at a late-night drug store, just in case I needed more money for cabfare.

I made it through Hell Week intact and enjoyed the remainder of my college years as a fraternity member. By the time I was in my junior year, I was elected chairman of the school dance committee. The unquestionable highlight of my experience was booking the famous Dorsey Brothers orchestra for our junior prom.

Like most people my age, I was a huge fan of the great swing orchestras that dominated American popular music during the 1930s and '40s. What a thrill it was to have three of the greatest swing musicians the world has ever known—Tommy Dorsey on trombone, Jimmy Dorsey on saxophone, and Helen O'Connor, the most famous big band singer of all time—playing at my college prom. We tore up the dance floor that night to songs like "One O'clock Jump" and "Song of India." I had booked all of them to play for a total of only $800.

Most of my time in college was spent working and studying, but Friday and Saturday nights were a different story. Those were sacred. From the day I turned eighteen until the day I met my future wife, I never let a Friday or Saturday night pass without going out on a date. I thought there was something the matter with you if you stayed home. Although I didn't smoke cigarettes, I always carried a pack of them in my jacket pocket when I went out on dates. I can't remember dating a girl who didn't ask for one. If you didn't have a pack with you, they thought you weren't smooth.

However, going out on the town required suitable attire, and this had always been a source of tremendous conflict between my father and me. The problem was that my father liked *everything* big: his house, his car, and *my clothes.* When my mother bought suits for me, he inspected them to make sure they were big enough. If the coat sleeves did not come down to the tips of my fingers, he would make her return the suit.

"It is lunacy to buy Stanford clothes that fit!" he roared. "He's only going to outgrow them in a few months. Buy clothes that are two sizes too big and he'll grow into them next year."

Somehow, when next year came along, my clothes still did not fit. It was embarrassing and when it came to my shoes, painful. My father only allowed me to wear high-top shoes. He believed that if I wore anything else, my ankles would catch a cold. (My father had a curious attitude toward illness. He insisted that whenever you got sick, it was your own fault for

J.C. with then-partner Grover Mendelsohn and Millard Newman at The Great Lakes Exposition, 1936, with miniature cigar factory

doing something wrong.) High-top shoes were not designed for skinny feet like mine and I always got sores from wearing them. They hurt me right to the bone. My father also liked me to wear spats. I had two pairs: one for daily use and another for holidays.

As a teenager I desperately wanted to buy a topcoat, a light coat suitable for spring, instead of the heavy winter coat my father insisted that I wear at all times.

"Topcoats are not practical," he said. "You either have a winter coat or you don't have any!"

If I could not persuade my father to buy me the clothes I wanted, I resolved to beat him on his own terms and buy them myself. I would show him I knew the value of a dollar.

As soon as I received my first paycheck as my father's downtown Cleveland salesman, I began scouring the newspaper for clothing advertisements. "Topcoats For Sale—Ten Dollars!" caught my eye and I was out the door. The store was far off in the outskirts of Cleveland. I had to transfer twice on the streetcar to get there. The neighborhood was a little scary, but I didn't care. With the first real money I ever made in the cigar business, I bought the first piece of clothing that ever fit me right.

When my father spotted me wearing my new topcoat, he was disgruntled. "Stanford, where did you get that coat?" he demanded to know.

"I bought it myself," I said with pride. It was my declaration of independence.

I continued to work part-time for my father for the rest of my college years. Over time I became a good salesman. So good, I earned up to twenty dollars a week on commission, an awful lot of money for a college student during the Depression, when twelve dollars a week was the average wage. I was one of the wealthiest kids in my college, and I tried to share my good fortune with my friends.

In the summer of 1936, my father arranged to give cigar-making demonstrations at the Great Lakes Exposition in Cleveland. This was a showcase for the most successful businesses in the Great Lakes states. J.C. had contracted to operate fourteen tobacco concession stands at the Exhibition Hall, but he was nervous about manning so many retail locations with his own salesmen. I solved the problem by recruiting my fraternity brothers to work the cigar stands. I gave them all a crash course in cigars and put them to work for thirty cents an hour.

They did a great job and they all made good money that summer. I was in their good graces for a while after that.

As my college days drew to a close, my future prospects for employment were very much on my mind. My father fully expected me to join the family business. It was what he had been grooming me for since childhood. I had learned a great deal about the business working part-time through college, not only from sales calls, but by meeting with distributors and leaf tobacco dealers and observing what went on in the factory.

However, I was concerned about working full-time for my father. As much as J.C. wanted his sons to carry on his legacy in the cigar business, he still expected to make all the decisions. How could I make my own mark on the company if he reserved all the control for himself? I would have to do battle with him over even the slightest changes I wanted to implement.

There was also the matter of the cigar business itself. I still didn't smoke cigars and wasn't sure I wanted to. Cigars seemed like an old man's pastime. Was there really a future for a young man like me in following my father's footsteps?

Public Square in Cleveland, c. 1920

CIGAR FAMILY

Millard and I
flank J.C. at the 1936
National Association of Tobacco
Distributors trade show

A HUNGARIAN IN CLEVELAND

*M*y father's feet often went shoeless when he was a child: not out of necessity, but because he loved to run barefoot through the tall grasses of the small peasant village of Koronch in Austria-Hungary where he grew up.

Julius Newman was born on May 26, 1875, into a large family of seven children who lived on the second floor of the only two-story brick building in the village, surrounded by acres of pastures and woods. Julius' father, Samuel, was the intellectual of the family, a religious scholar who earned his living traveling the countryside as a teacher of the Talmud. It fell to Julius's mother, Hannah, whom my father affectionately called "the boss," to run the Newman household. She also ran the village tavern and a store situated on the ground floor of the Newman home, the same house where she had been born and raised. Hannah was a formidable woman with a stout body and a stern demeanor who made all the important decisions in the family. I have no doubt that my father inherited both his imperious nature and his business skills from her.

The Newmans made an adequate living in Koronch, where they raised chickens, ducks, geese, and cows, and grew their own vegetables. However, as a Jewish family in late nineteenth-century Hungary, they were forbidden by law to own land or to vote. Count Andrashy, an absentee landlord who also happened to be the Prime Minister of Hungary, owned the entire village. This left a strong impression on my father, who later expressed his freedom in America by accumulating real estate and political connections with a vengeance.

It was also in Hungary that cigars first caught my father's attention. Every January, Julius marched with the local schoolchildren in an annual pilgrimage to Count Andrashy's palace in the nearby town of Terebash, to serenade Andrashy's wife, the Countess Katherine, on the occasion of her birthday. As Julius raised his voice in song to the strains of the national anthem, "God Bless All Hungarians," he was mesmerized by the sight of the Countess, listening from the veranda of her palace, smoking a long black cigar.

For a time, the Newmans were content with their life in Koronch. However, conditions under the feudal system were becoming increasingly oppressive. Religious and social discrimination was intensifying throughout the Austro-Hungarian Empire and Hannah's sons were at constant risk of conscription into the army. The Newmans watched as one by one, relatives and friends abandoned their homeland and emigrated to America. By 1887, Hannah Newman had decided it was time for her family to join the tide. Before uprooting her entire family, she sent Samuel off with their eleven-year-old son, Max, on an exploratory trip to the United States. Samuel would visit relatives in Cleveland and Chicago and report back to her on their prospects in the New World.

Samuel liked Chicago, but it was Cleveland that impressed him the most. A major inland port city on Lake Erie, divided by the Cuyahoga River, Cleveland had easy access to iron ore, limestone, and coal, making the city one of the country's principal steel manufacturing centers

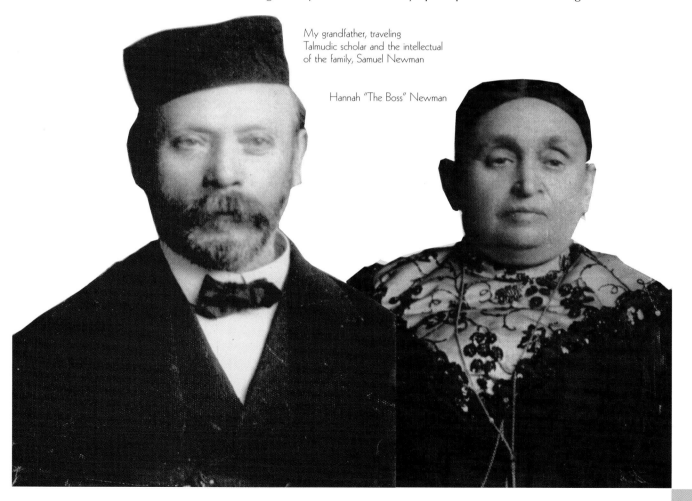

My grandfather, traveling Talmudic scholar and the intellectual of the family, Samuel Newman

Hannah "The Boss" Newman

Back row: Morris, Julius, Pauline, Max, Mitchell; Front row: Lena, Samuel, Hannah, and Isaac

and attracting thousands of immigrants. More than one-third of Cleveland's population was Polish, Italian, Czech, German, Irish, and Hungarian immigrants who had established their own neighborhoods near the factories where they worked.

Samuel returned to Koronch and told Hannah that Cleveland was a suitable place to begin a new life. He then brought his three eldest sons, Isaac, Morris, and Max, back to Cleveland where they acquired a house and prepared for the arrival of the rest of the family.

In October of 1888, Julius said goodbye to the old country forever. Packing only some clothing and a few small heirlooms, Hannah Newman shepherded Julius, his youngest brother, Mitchell, and his two sisters, Lena and Pauline, to the Koronch train station where they boarded a train to Bremen, Germany. At the bustling Bremen seaport, crowded with thousands upon thousands of immigrants, they departed on a ship bound for Baltimore, Maryland.

CIGAR FAMILY

My father never tired of telling me the story of his voyage across the cold North Atlantic. It was an agonizing experience for the thirteen-year-old boy. He had never traveled by sea before and the ship was tossed back and forth so violently that he was seasick throughout the entire two-week crossing. The family subsisted on a constant diet of pickled herring, which only compounded my father's misery. He developed an intense hatred of pickled herring during those two weeks and wouldn't touch it for years thereafter.

My father was immensely relieved upon finally setting foot in America. It was unlike anything he had seen before. He was especially impressed by how slender and well-dressed everyone looked. Surely this was a land of opportunity. Julius was treated to his first taste of bananas and sweet rolls, and thought they were the most delicious things he had ever eaten. They were certainly better than the pickled herring. He was so excited by America and the prospect of his impending family reunion that he could hardly sleep on the night train from Baltimore to Cleveland.

Hannah and her children arrived at the Cleveland train station on a bright Sunday morning. Samuel and his sons were waiting for them on the platform. Everyone embraced and together they set off for their new home. My father's elation at being reunited with his father and brothers began to subside as the family made its way through the congested streets of Cleveland, a bustling metropolis crowded with towering smokestacks, as different from their former home in the Hungarian countryside as one could imagine. It was a difficult adjustment for a family who already missed the sights and smells of forest and field. It was particularly confining to my father, who could no longer walk freely without shoes. His disappointment reached its peak when the family arrived at the tiny house Samuel had acquired. It was pitifully small for nine people.

Not to be discouraged, Hannah quickly set about improving the situation. Within a few months of her arrival in Cleveland she had pooled the family's resources and moved them into a much larger home on a bigger plot of land. Much to my father's delight, the property included a barn. The family purchased a few farm animals and planted a garden, restoring some semblance of the life they had left behind.

Hannah was determined to make the most of their new life, which meant finding suitable professions for her sons. Her daughters were expected to stay home to take care of the housework. After evaluating the employment situation, she decided that Cleveland's rapidly growing garment industry held great promise for her sons.

In contrast to Europe, where most clothing was still made by hand in the home, machine-made clothing was an emerging phenomenon in America. Anyone who wanted to join a profession first had to spend three years in apprenticeship to a master tradesman and Hannah soon found one to train her eldest son, Isaac, as a custom tailor. Isaac learned fast and eventually opened one of Cleveland's first ready-to-wear clothing factories, producing some of the finest women's clothing in town.

Morris and Max also embarked on careers in the garment industry, although they ultimately went into the insurance business. Mitchell was a successful tailor until the early 1920s, when his life was tragically cut short. He suffered from diabetes and was rushed to the hospital one day following an attack, where he died from an overdose of insulin. Had the doctors understood diabetes better in those days, they could have prevented his death simply by giving him a lump of sugar to counteract the overdose.

Hannah chose a different profession for my father. The cigar trade was popular among Hungarians in Cleveland. In fact, several of Cleveland's cigar factories were owned by Hungarians. Hannah had a few friends whose children worked as cigarmakers and she was able to arrange an apprenticeship for my father, for which she paid three dollars a month for the next three years.

The cigar profession commanded a fair amount of prestige at the turn of the century. Cigars were arguably the most popular tobacco product in America. Almost every city in the East and Midwest had at least one small cigar factory. Cigarmakers were highly regarded for their craftsmanship and carried themselves with great dignity. Cigarmakers took pride in their appearance, always traveling to and from work in a hat, suit, and tie, changing into less fancy clothes for the factory floor. All this undoubtedly appealed to my father.

Julius learned his trade by day and studied English and American history at night school. Much of his apprenticeship was spent sweeping floors and hauling coal and beer to warm the cigarmakers on the factory floor. Most of his fellow cigar apprentices were also in their early to mid-teens.

Starting to work in the factory around seven or eight in the morning, cigarmakers donned a long apron and proceeded to their cigar tables on the cigar floor. The floor was a large gallery filled with benches and worktables. Each cigarmaker sat at the same bench every day. They needed as much natural light as possible to scrutinize the tobacco, so most factories had tall windows on all four sides. The windows were usually closed to prevent fresh air from drying out the tobacco, which concentrated the tobacco smell to such an extent on the factory floor that the affect could be overpowering. It also made things very hot and humid. On top of that, the factory floor was a noisy place to work, with the cigarmakers carrying on heated discussions about the political issues of the day.

Julius began his apprenticeship by watching the cigarmakers demonstrate how to make cigars. In time, he was "working up" his own tobacco, as the process was known. He first placed a binder leaf on his cigar board—the cigarmaker's most basic tool. He then gathered different pieces of filler tobacco in the palm of his left hand, breaking them off at a uniform length. Once he had shaped the filler, he rolled it up inside his binder leaf, creating the bunch. The foreman would inspect his work and point out where Julius had made a wrong twist or crossed too many filler leaves at one point. This blocked the smoke and prevented a smooth draw. He was also criticized if he packed the bunch too loosely, which allowed too much air to pass through the cigar too quickly, resulting in too hot a burn.

The last step was to select an outer wrapper leaf, stretch it out over the board, cut it to the proper shape and, beginning at the "tuck" (the lighting end of the cigar), roll the bunch inside the wrapper in a spiral motion. Wrapper leaf has always been the most expensive type of tobacco used in cigar making. Unlike filler tobacco, which is rough, wrapper tobacco is cultivated to be smooth and stretchable, like silk, and has a strong influence on the taste and appearance of the cigar. Therefore, Julius was expected to get several cuts out of each wrapper leaf.

The hardest part was making sure all his cigars were uniform in appearance, size, shape, and weight. He started making the cheapest cigars and worked his way up to the better grades. In his last year of apprenticeship, he worked right on the floor among the cigarmakers to learn speed. Cigarmakers averaged two to four hundred cigars a day. Truly exceptional speed was considered a natural gift that could not be taught.

Upon completing his long and costly apprenticeship, my father was finally qualified as a union journeyman cigarmaker and worked steadily for the next six months. Then the Panic of 1893 struck. This nationwide financial crisis forced even the most experienced cigarmakers out of work. There was little hope for an eighteen-year-old novice. Julius was unemployed for the next two years. As he later told me, "I couldn't *buy* a job."

At one point during this difficult time, my father left Cleveland to look for work in New York City. As a union journeyman cigarmaker, he was qualified to practice his trade at any union cigar factory in the country. Shortly after arriving in the Big Apple, he located a cigar factory and was hired on the spot to start work the next day. Thrilled at his change of fortune, my father found his way back to wherever he was staying for the night, probably a flophouse, and slept peacefully. He rose bright and early the next morning, eager to start his new job.

Stepping out into the crowded streets of New York, my father stopped dead in his tracks as he realized, much to his chagrin, that he could not remember his way back to the cigar factory. He searched in vain for the next three days, but no matter how many times he tried to retrace his steps, he kept getting lost in the maze of Manhattan. He finally gave up and returned to Cleveland, where the employment situation remained bleak.

Desperate for work, Julius decided to go into business for himself as a "buckeye" cigarmaker. The name buckeye was used in the cigar industry to denote a small cigar shop that commonly used tobacco grown in Ohio, the Buckeye State. (Buckeyes are a type of chestnut prevalent in Ohio.) Most of Cleveland's cigar factories were situated along a street called Buckeye Road, not far from the Hungarian neighborhood. Buckeyes worked long hours, paid more for tobacco than larger manufacturers who could buy in bulk, and obtained most of their orders from saloonkeepers who pressured them to patronize their saloons in exchange for their business. Becoming a buckeye was a daunting proposition for Julius. Where would he find his first customer? Once again, Hannah Newman took charge.

"I will take you to where I buy my groceries," she decided. "I am certain I can persuade our grocer to buy some of your cigars."

Upon visiting the family grocer, Hannah did all the talking. "I come here every day to buy bread and milk and everything else for my family," she said. "You make a good business from us. Now I want you to do something for me in return. I know that you sell a great many cigars in your establishment. As it happens, my son is an experienced cigarmaker. He is just starting his own business and it would be a great help if you would place an order with him. Shall we say 500 cigars?"

Refusing Hannah Newman would not have been worth the aggravation. The grocer agreed and Julius was on his way.

My father's next step was to apply for a federal license to work as an independent cigarmaker. Licenses were required because the federal government taxed cigars. Julius had to buy excise tax stamps at the post office to paste on all of his cigar boxes. It was against the law to sell a box of cigars without the proper stamps. Finally, he borrowed fifty dollars from his family and purchased two bundles of tobacco.

In my father's day, most cigar manufacturers purchased their tobacco from leaf tobacco dealers, brokers, and packers: middlemen who offered different types of tobacco from all over the world. Manufacturers would buy from local dealers—Water Street in New York City was home to at least thirty of them—or from traveling salesmen who went from city to city with suitcases full of tobacco samples to show. Now that the thousands of small cigar manufacturers are gone, the few large cigar manufacturers remaining today mostly buy tobacco directly from growers, and most of the dealers who were once a fixture of life in the industry have almost completely disappeared, with a few exceptions.

Having purchased his first bundles of tobacco from a local dealer, my father fashioned a cigar table out of some old boards and converted the family barn into a one-man cigar factory. On May 5, 1895, Julius Newman rolled his first cigars as a buckeye cigarmaker. J.C.

The humble beginnings of J.C. Newman Cigar Co., circa 1895

Newman Cigar Company was now one of the 42,000 federally registered cigar manufacturers in the United States, and in direct competition with 300 registered cigar factories in Cleveland.

In contrast to the crowded cigar factory where my father learned his trade, the barn must have been a lonely place to work. At least he had a few farm animals for company. I can picture him taking a break from his cigar making every morning to milk the cows. More than a few relatives were "invited" to the barn to help strip stems from tobacco leaves.

My father's business expanded quickly from these humble beginnings. His first substantial order—for 10,000 cigars—came from the William Edwards Company, one of the largest wholesale grocers in Cleveland. Wholesale grocers were significant distributors of cigars in those days. According to my father, the order was recorded by John D. Rockefeller, one of William Edwards' bookkeepers at the time. Rockefeller, of course, went on to become one of the richest men in America, amassing a huge fortune with Standard Oil Company in Cleveland.

Julius' order for 10,000 cigars was more than he had dared to hope for—or that he could possibly meet by himself—and he hired a few of his unemployed cigarmaker friends to help fill it. My father was always grateful to the William Edwards Company, which remained a loyal customer for the next fifty-five years.

My father was a good talker and he kept the orders coming. He printed up business cards, but soon threw them all away. He found that some saloonkeepers would place orders and then cancel them the next week. Without a business card from J.C. Newman, they had no way of contacting him to cancel. Some saloonkeepers became quite angry when they realized they couldn't cancel their orders. My father appeased them by buying drinks for everyone when he visited their establishments.

As fall turned to winter, Cleveland's heavy snows made the unheated barn an impossibly cold place to roll cigars. Julius moved his operation into the house and stored his tobacco in Hannah's fruit cellar. This caused an unexpected problem when one day, as the family gathered around the breakfast table, Hannah opened a jar of preserves and wrinkled her nose in disgust. She took a small taste and grimaced again.

"There is something wrong with this jam," she said. "Who has been tampering with my preserves?" When no one replied, she proceeded downstairs to investigate. Opening the door of her fruit cellar, that strange smell wafted out. She immediately recognized the source: It was coming from her son's tobacco. That was the end of that.

"Julius, it is time you found a place of business outside this house," she said.

There was no arguing with Hannah. My father was compelled to lease his first store, for which he somewhat anxiously paid $20 a month. He need not have worried. His business continued to expand, allowing him to lease a larger space and hire a few more cigarmakers.

In 1898, the Spanish-American War was declared. My father, a true patriot, prepared to close his business and join the war effort. He wrote a letter volunteering his services to a young assistant secretary of the Navy named Teddy Roosevelt, who was forming a volunteer group called the Rough Riders to help Cuba fight for its independence from Spain. By the time my father's request was processed, the war was over.

Meanwhile, my father's business continued to grow. I once asked him how he was able to build his business having started with so little capital.

"I purchased my raw materials from suppliers who had money and could afford to give me extended credit, sometimes a year," he explained. "And I sold my cigars to customers who could pay me immediately. That is how I built up sufficient capital to expand my business."

At first, he could only afford to produce generic cigars with stock labels provided by his customers, similar to today's private label products. His first exclusive cigar brand was inspired by the Cleveland streetcar, a fixture of life in the city and a particularly impressive one for the young Hungarian immigrant. He named his first cigar brand A-B-C after the interurban streetcar line that serviced Cleveland and its neighboring suburbs of Akron and Bedford. It was the same streetcar I later took to buy my first topcoat.

Three years after introducing A-B-C, my father introduced the Dr. Nichol brand. Its label featured a white-bearded doctor with the caption, "One after each meal, or oftener, if desired." Dr. Nichol was made with domestic filler tobacco from Ohio and Pennsylvania, with a wrapper imported from Sumatra in the East Indies. Dr. Nichol became so closely associated with my father that customers would come to his factory expecting to meet the famous white-haired doctor. They were shocked to find a clean-shaven young man in his twenties running the place.

Judge Wright was probably the most enduring of all the brands my father introduced. Its success was due largely to its fine-tasting Connecticut Broadleaf wrapper. The Judge Wright label pictured a distinguished judge above the slogan, "A fair trial will give a verdict in favor of this cigar." Cleveland's verdict on Judge Wright was to make it the most popular five-cent cigar in town. It continued to sell well into the 1950s.

The five-cent cigar was an institution in those days, like the five-cent loaf of bread, candy bar, Coca-Cola, or bottle of milk. It was not easy to produce a quality cigar at that price, especially with the high cost of union cigarmakers. As a result, more and more cigar manufacturers began training women to make cigars. Women were not customarily in the union and therefore, were not paid as much as union cigarmakers.

By 1905, my father, now going by his new initials, J.C., realized that his union cigar factory in Cleveland could no longer operate profitably. As an experiment, he opened a new non-union factory on the other side of town staffed almost entirely by women. This new factory proved so successful that he closed his union factory and concentrated his efforts on the new operation.

In 1909, J.C. decided it was time to find a bride. As he put it, "Suddenly, I found myself thirty-three years old and unmarried. I felt that if I waited much longer to marry, I'd be shelved."

A 1950s version of the label with the original "Fair Trial" slogan

CIGAR FAMILY

J.C. receives an award from the Brand Names Foundation for his Judge Wright brand in 1949

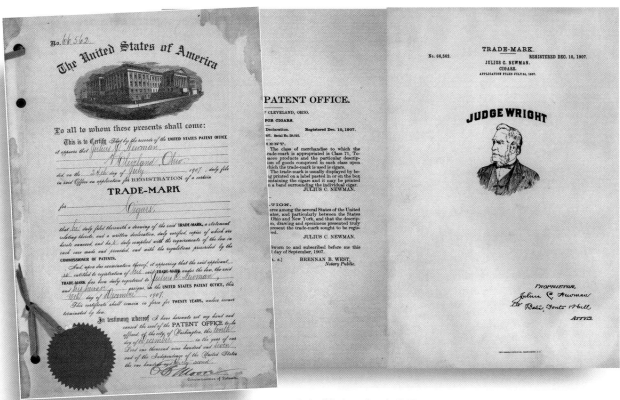

Judge Wright trademark, 1907

My father (in center wearing Derby hat) and his employees in front of J.C. Newman Cigar Co.'s Cleveland factory in 1905, after just ten years in business

He asked his friends and relatives to recommend suitable single women. Whenever he received the name and address of an eligible young lady, he made sure one of his business trips took him to her town. It was during one of these business trips that my father found the girl of his dreams in a prominent Detroit family whose ancestors had also come from Austria-Hungary.

Gladys Pollasky was a beautiful twenty-one-year-old woman with auburn hair. My father called on her one Saturday afternoon, introducing himself as a distant relative to get his foot in the door. He had some difficulty explaining just how they were related, but they enjoyed each other's company and he asked if he could meet her parents the next day. She agreed.

J.C. was fascinated upon meeting Mr. and Mrs. Max Pollasky to learn about their distinguished family heritage. Gladys' grandfather had been a pioneer settler during the covered wagon days. He had received a land grant in northern Michigan and searched for his land for days in the Michigan wilds. Finally, exhausted and discouraged, he and his family camped by a river to rest for the Sabbath. The next morning, visitors on horseback arrived and told them the very river beside which they had made camp was on their own land. In

CIGAR FAMILY

Gladys Pollasky at 18

time, with the help of other settlers, they founded the town of Alma, Michigan, now a city of 20,000 inhabitants and home of a respected university.

My father made up his mind that he had better land this special girl quickly, "while she was still fresh out of school and before she had a chance to get too well acquainted with any competitors!" After a period of courtship, he proposed marriage.

One day when I was poking around a cubbyhole next to our ballroom, I found some of the love letters my father had written to her during their courtship, tucked away inside a felt bag my mother owned. I sat down right there and read for two hours. My father had been very impressed by Gladys Pollasky and her family's position in Detroit society. He thought he was marrying the Queen of Sheba. In return, he spared no expense trying to impress the Pollaskys.

On my father's wedding day, April 21, 1909, he arrived in style at the Detroit train station in a private railway car.

Before he disembarked, a five-piece band emerged from his car and began to play. A red carpet was unfurled and out stepped J.C. Newman and his entourage to the applause of the Pollasky family waiting on the platform.

With his family life established, my father redoubled his efforts to expand his business. In 1914, after the birth of my sisters, Helen and Elaine, he custom-built his largest factory yet. The 50,000 square foot building at 38th Street and Woodland Avenue was now the largest cigar factory in Cleveland. Things went so well, he was able to open two more factories in the neighboring towns of Marion and Lorain, Ohio.

During this time, J.C.'s brother, Max, who had made a successful career in insurance after leaving the garment industry, approached my father about investing in a life insurance policy. Max worked for the Massachusetts Mutual Life Insurance Company and wanted to be part of the company's Million Dollar Roundtable, an elite group of top salesmen who sold a million dollars' worth of insurance every year. J.C. agreed to help his brother out, and purchased a great deal of life insurance over the years to help keep Max in the Million Dollar Roundtable.

Opposite Top:
The Pollasky family of Detroit, Michigan (1908)
Back: Cecelia and Max; Front: Norman, Gladys, Vera, and Nelson

Opposite Bottom:
J.C.'s new factory in Marion, Ohio (1914)

·CIGAR·FACTORY·BLDG·BRANCH·N°2·   ·J·C· NEWMAN· CIGAR· CO·   ·MARION· OHIO·
FULTON & TAYLOR· ARCHITECTS·
·CLEVELAND· OHIO·

Just when J.C. felt things were proceeding nicely, World War I erupted, creating severe shortages of people and materials. Skilled cigarmakers either left the cigar business for more lucrative war-related industries or were drafted into the military. Moreover, Hungarian immigrants, who constituted a majority of J.C.'s workforce, stopped coming to America during the war. Paper for cigar labels and wood for cigar boxes also became scarce, and cigar taxes rose to astronomical heights.

My father trusted in technology to offset the difficulties imposed by the war, and in 1916 purchased some of the industry's first cigar machines from American Machine & Foundry (AMF). To the best of my knowledge, only one or two other manufacturers were using cigar machines at the time.

A long filler cigar machine, recently developed by AMF, was modeled after handmade operations. The machine required four operators, including a filler feeder and a binder layer. The technology was less than perfect: Cigar machinery was in its infancy during World War I.

My father sent his head mechanic to visit AMF in New York City to learn how to operate the machines. The mechanic was supposed to return to Cleveland to instruct my father's cigarmakers. Unfortunately, he liked his new surroundings so much that he decided to stay in New York. Consequently, when the cigar machines arrived at the factory in Marion, Ohio, no one knew how to operate them properly. Reluctantly, my father instructed his workers to do their best. The task was beyond them. Thousands of poorly made cigars were returned by irate storeowners who questioned J.C.'s ability as a cigar manufacturer.

In a desperate attempt to salvage his reputation, my father threw more money at the problem and ordered upgraded machines from AMF, insisting that the company send its best mechanic to train his operators. By the time the new machines arrived in 1919, it was too late. A recession hit the cigar industry and J.C. was forced to sell all his machines at a substantial loss.

The financial crisis of 1920 pulled the rug out from under many industries. Inventory values dropped over fifty percent. The most serious problem for the cigar industry was that in the 1920s, cigarettes became more popular than cigars for the first time in history. This happened due to the fact that the Red Cross had supplied millions of cigarettes to American soldiers during World War I. Many a soldier returned from Europe with a new taste for cigarettes.

My father was forced to close his factories in Marion and Lorain. The Cleveland factory, his pride and joy, faced bankruptcy. I was about four years old at the time and I can still remember my father getting into his car every morning and selling cigars door-to-door, just as he had done in the old days. It was as if he were starting all over again.

In the nick of time, Uncle Max reminded my father about those insurance policies he had so generously purchased to keep his brother in the Million Dollar Roundtable. Their accumulated value was now over half a million dollars. After J.C. cashed his policies, his first priority was to pay off all his creditors. That didn't leave much money left over, but as he told me later, "At least I didn't owe anybody—and I never filed for bankruptcy."

I often overheard my father bragging to our customers that we never had a fire. The meaning behind this stems from the tough times in 1920 and later during the Great Depression, when manufacturers would burn down their own factories to collect insurance. My father was proud that he had never been reduced to such desperate measures.

Throughout this entire ordeal, one brand more than any other kept the company afloat. John Carver, which J.C. had introduced in 1917, was consistently one of the best-selling

nickel cigars in the Midwest. Named after the first governor of Plymouth Colony, John Carver helped J.C. Newman Cigar Company maintain a foothold in the depressed cigar market of the 1920s.

Business was not my father's only concern during World War I. Food was scarce. Basic commodities like potatoes practically disappeared from the market. President Woodrow Wilson appealed to all citizens to plant victory gardens to meet this emergency. J.C. leased a sixty-acre farm and provided milk and potatoes to his employees for the duration of the war. He always considered his employees part of the family, a belief I wholeheartedly adopted when I joined the business. My father also remembered his origins and brought several families of European refugees across the Atlantic to start a new life in America.

It's an old cliché, but cigars and politics do go hand in hand, or at least they still did in those days. My father had quite a few photographs of himself posing with various politicians. I once asked him why all the men in his pictures had such large bellies. "That's to show how prosperous they are," he said. He sported a sizable potbelly himself and was proud of it.

My father met and courted many local politicians in the saloons of Cleveland. He used to laugh about the extravagant political promises he overheard in the saloons, few of which were ever carried out. Nonetheless, he was a good friend to the politicians he believed in. He solicited votes for his favorites when making his rounds, including Newton Baker, who became mayor of Cleveland. President Woodrow Wilson later appointed Baker his Secretary of War. My father also became friendly with Cleveland Mayor Harold Burton, who went on to become Chief Justice of the Ohio Supreme Court. In time, my father's political connections reached the highest office in the land.

In 1914, he helped form the Young Men's Republican Club in Cleveland. A few years later, he met Ohio Senator Warren G. Harding, who was a member of the Marion Chamber of Commerce, which had helped my father purchase his factory there. Harding was an avid cigar smoker, and he and J.C. became friends. Perhaps one of the things they had in common, besides their love of cigars, was that they had both defied the odds to establish their own businesses.

Some of the industry's first cigar machines being used
by J.C.'s all-female workforce

J.C. presenting cigars to Supreme Court Justice Harold Burton

Early in his career, Harding had purchased a bankrupt daily newspaper, the *Marion Star*, and did every job himself—writing editorials, selling advertising, even washing ink rollers—to turn it into a success, much as my father had done every job imaginable to get his cigar business off the ground.

J.C. was so taken with Harding that he helped establish the first Harding Republican Club. In his own small way, he helped Harding become the twenty-ninth President of the United States. Harding was elected in 1920 on a promise of a "return to normalcy" after the hardships of World War I. He was a popular president whose reputation was unfortunately tarnished by scandal. Teapot Dome was the most notorious scandal of Harding's presidency. It involved Harding's Secretary of the Interior, who granted drilling rights in Naval oil reserves to his friends in exchange for kickbacks. Historians now believe Harding was innocent of any wrongdoing, except perhaps in his poor choice of cabinet members.

Installed in Washington, the Hardings opened the gates of their new home and welcomed their friends and supporters. My parents attended his Inaugural Ball and later visited the First Family at the White House in 1923. My mother told the President, "You live in such a lovely house," to which Harding replied, "It's not my house, it's yours. The White House belongs to you and everyone in the United States." My father took great pride in keeping the president supplied with cigars until Harding's untimely death that same year, while Harding was still in the middle of his term.

As the Roaring Twenties continued, my father survived the rapid concentration of the cigar industry into fewer and fewer hands. By 1927, his was one of just two cigar companies remaining in the city of Cleveland. The other was Mendelsohn Cigar Company, which owned the popular Rigoletto and Student Prince brands, both named after popular operettas of the day. A merger of the two survivors made sense. Each had a good sales organization and popular brands. Together, they could save on office space and create synergies in manufacturing and distribution. In 1927, when I was eleven years old, J.C. Newman Cigar Company joined with Mendelsohn Cigar Company to form Cleveland's sole cigar company.

Grover Mendelsohn, my father's new partner, was a friendly, good-looking fellow and an excellent salesman. He was a talented musician who could play the piano by ear. He was also something of a ladies' man, despite the fact that he was married. He was certainly vain, because he insisted that his name come first in the newly merged cigar company. Thus, Mendelsohn & Newman Cigar Manufacturers was born.

My father didn't care whether his name came first or second, as long as he was named president of the company. Eventually, the company name was shortened to M & N Cigar Manufacturers and, as my father put it: "Grover got to be 'M'. I got to be president."

M & N became a major force in the marketplace, but my father could not enjoy his new-found sense of security for long. In just two years, the Great Depression hit. Hundreds of competitors closed, but this only benefited those who could stay solvent. Most cigar manufacturers were forced to cut prices in half.

How did my father survive while so many of his competitors failed? He had the spirit of a true pioneer, and that made all the difference. He was always on the cutting edge, always willing to try new things, never willing to give up.

For example, J.C. was a true believer in the benefits of advertising. He always employed an ad agency, even during the Great Depression, when advertising was considered a luxury by many. As sporting events began to play an increasingly prominent role in American life, he advertised Student Prince cigars in Cleveland Indians baseball programs, sponsored intermission shows at Cleveland Barons hockey games, and gave away free boxes of cigars to every golfer making a hole-in-one at any of Cleveland's municipal golf courses.

My father was also quick to embrace new innovations. Just prior to the Depression, he had become the first in the industry to individually wrap cigars in cellophane. Cigars had been in great need of a new kind of packaging in the late 1920s. The Package Machinery Company had introduced a machine in 1918 that encased cigars in a foil wrapper, and this had become a popular method of packaging cigars for several years. However, while foil helped protect cigars, it also prevented consumers from seeing what was inside. Too often, when smokers removed the foil, they discovered damaged or off-colored cigars inside. By 1925, the public had refused to buy cigars encased in foil.

My father was well aware of the problem. In 1927, a local company that made cellophane bags for peanuts approached him about packaging multiple cigars in cellophane pouches; he immediately recognized the potential in cellophane. It would help protect cigars from drying out, while allowing consumers to see what they were getting. However, he did not like the

Cleveland Indians baseball game program, 1932

Rigoletto advertisement, 1911

A sales meeting in 1935. From right to left starting at middle of head table: J.C., Lillian, and Grover Mendelsohn (Stanford third from left in front)

idea of placing several cigars in a cellophane bag. He felt the best way to protect and present cigars would be to cellophane them individually. Thus, Student Prince became the first cigar in the industry to be individually wrapped in cellophane. Individually cellophaning cigars soon became standard practice throughout the cigar industry.

Perhaps the most significant reason for M & N's survival during the Great Depression was my father's decision to transform the business from a handmade to a machine-made operation. As the high cost of hand-rolling cigars became prohibitive, more and more large manufacturers were converting to machinery. In 1926, machine-made cigars had accounted for a mere eighteen percent of the American cigar industry. By 1936, machine-made cigars constituted a whopping seventy-five percent of the market.

Finding the right cigar machines at the right price was critical. My father had not forgotten his disastrous first experience with AMF and turned instead to one of their chief competitors, the

CIGAR FAMILY

Arenco Machine Company of Sweden. Arenco's short filler cigar machines required two operators, and produced from 4,000 to 5,000 cigars a day, depending upon the the skill of the operators. In 1932, my father purchased twenty-four of these short filler cigar machines and installed them in a huge, modern cigar factory he had recently acquired from one of the nation's leading cigar companies, the American Cigar Company in Cleveland. (Incidentally, when this factory was eventually demolished, the property on which it once stood became the site of Jacob's Field, the present home of the Cleveland Indians.)

My father now focused all his attention on finding the perfect use for his new machines. Creating a new cigar brand was out of the question. Introducing a new brand name was a huge challenge. It still is today, especially in the cigar industry. Smokers usually remained loyal to their favorite cigar brands, regardless of what company manufactured them, and it was a common practice for cigar manufacturers to buy or trade popular brand registrations. One of J.C.'s most successful business tactics was to purchase popular cigar brands from factories that went out of business. One of these, Cameo, he had purchased several years earlier, and it was still familiar to cigar smokers. With his new cigar machines cranked up to full capacity in his brand-new factory, my father introduced Little Cameo, one of the first machine-made small cigars in America, and the first little cigar to be individually banded and cellophaned.

Retailing for just two cents each, Little Cameo was a huge success. M & N received so many orders that my father was able to employ more than 200 cigar machine operators six days a week, two shifts a day. M & N turned out 120,000 Little Cameos daily, which still wasn't enough to meet the demand.

However, my father made little profit on these cigars because they sold for a very low price. He needed some help from Uncle Sam for additional working capital. He applied for and received a government loan to help his business through the Depression. As was typical of my father, he repaid the loan in full, well before it was due. The government was so impressed they offered him a second loan. My father politely refused, saying he was glad he didn't need it.

J.C. Newman persevered even when those around him wanted to give up. In the fall of 1933, I was sitting in his office one Saturday afternoon (we always worked a half-day on Saturdays) when a group of factory foremen stormed into the office. They were up in arms that President Roosevelt had just established the country's first minimum wage of twenty-five cents an hour. My father's foremen were appalled. They felt the minimum wage would destroy us. Cigarmakers had always been paid by piecework; that is, by the number of cigars they produced each week. The foremen were convinced that by guaranteeing workers a minimum salary regardless of the number of cigars they produced, they would inevitably produce fewer cigars. A heated discussion ensued, the foremen insisting that our only recourse was to liquidate the business immediately.

My father was not one to throw in the towel. He decided to pay the twenty-five cents an hour and see it through. Once he made up his mind, you couldn't change it. No matter what anyone said—and there were a lot of strong words exchanged that Saturday afternoon—when my father decided to do something, he did it. He convinced his foremen to stay the course, and it all worked out in the end. Even when Washington raised the minimum wage to thirty cents the next year, cigarmakers still produced enough cigars to offset the cost of their minimum wage.

I witnessed many of these ups and downs firsthand. What I hadn't seen up close, my father told me about on our long walks in the evenings after dinner. It took a great deal of stamina just to survive in the cigar industry, let alone expand your business. My father was perfectly suited to it. He rose to each new challenge with seemingly endless reserves of energy and ingenuity. He had a sixth sense about the cigar business and always seemed to know what to do next. Following in his footsteps would be a challenge.

T HE WAR YEARS

CHAPTER **3**

On Memorial Day 1938, I came home to find Grover Mendelsohn sitting with my father on our front porch. Grover's wife, Lillian, had recently paid my father a surprise visit while Grover was away on one of his long business trips. Lillian was a beautiful lady, but she could be rather headstrong. You only had to spend five minutes with her to see that she must have been difficult to get along with. Grover was only too happy to extend his business trips as long as possible to stay away from her and have some fun on the road. This time, his reputation as a ladies' man had caught up with him.

"Lillian came by to talk to me the other day," my father said.

"What on earth did she want?" Grover asked.

"I don't know how to tell you this, so I'll be blunt. She said she was filing for a divorce. I told her I was sorry to hear it, but I couldn't see what that had to do with me. She reminded me that her father had loaned you money when we first formed the company and that he took your stock as collateral. She claims that you never paid him back and when he died, she inherited the stock. Now she wants to sell it."

Grover looked a little pale, but his voice remained calm as he asked, "What did you do?"

"At first I was too stunned to reply. Then she said, 'Look, if you don't buy my stock, I'll just sell it to somebody else. Do you want it or not?'"

My father paused.

"Grover, I could not let our stock get into the hands of a competitor. I agreed to buy it."

Grover just sat there for a minute soaking it all in.

"That's okay," he finally said. "I understand."

My father quickly added, "You are more than welcome to stay with the company in your present position at your current salary."

"Thanks but no thanks," Grover said. "My wife has sold me down the river! I don't want to have anything to do with her or the business. I appreciate the offer, but I'm leaving and I'm not coming back. I'll work for another company in some other town. Believe me, I've had offers."

Thus the "M" in M & N left the company for good and J.C. Newman became its sole owner. It was a memorable Memorial Day. Grover ended up working for his relatives' cigar company in Philadelphia. He and my father remained on good terms and continued to consult with each other from time to time.

I graduated from Western Reserve University three weeks later. In the three years I had served as M & N's downtown Cleveland salesman, I had learned a great deal about the cigar business. I had a pretty good idea of what I would be getting myself into by joining my father's company full-time. I was definitely interested in the financial side of the business. With all the accounting courses I had taken at Western Reserve, I could have sat for the CPA exam in another six months and become a certified public accountant. My father said there was no time for that. He wanted me to join M & N immediately.

I was lucky I had the option. Friends of mine who graduated at the same time I did were having difficulty finding work. Joe Babin was one of my best friends. He was very bright, received excellent grades, graduated cum laude from law school, and couldn't find a decent job. He visited practically every law firm in Cleveland, and the most they were offering was $15 a week writing legal briefs. I made more than that working part-time for my father.

"I can't live on $15 a week," Joe told me. He wanted to get married and needed a decent income to start a family.

"Why don't you go work for your father?" I asked. I was half kidding, because I knew Joe and his father didn't get along all that well. Joe's father owned a successful sash and door business, but Joe did everything he could to avoid working there. He preferred working for my father during the summers at the Cleveland Exposition.

In the end, Joe joined his dad's company after all. The job market was so bad that it looked like I would have to do the same thing, but I still needed a little convincing. My father thought a trip around the country to meet with some of his distributors and suppliers would do the trick. He would show me what a great business the cigar industry was.

His plan almost backfired. On more than one occasion, one of my father's own contacts pulled me aside and warned me not to get into the cigar business.

"A bright young fellow like you should be doing something else," they told me, well out of earshot of my father. "Only old men smoke cigars. What happens to your business when all the old men die off? In five years you won't have a business."

A callous way of putting it, but a valid question nonetheless. By now, I wasn't afraid to confront my father about anything, so I told him what his peers had said and asked him what he thought about it.

"Son, don't worry," he said. "Every few years, new old men come along."

Not quite the answer I was looking for.

We embarked on the next leg of our trip, which I had been looking forward to with great anticipation: my first visit to Cuba. Getting there by ship was an ordeal. The ocean was so turbulent that most of the passengers spent the entire voyage from Miami to Havana hanging over the rail, throwing up into the sea. When we finally got back on solid ground, I asked one of the seasick passengers, "How did you enjoy the trip?"

A young professional

"When I purchased my ticket to Havana, I didn't realize I would be traveling *by rail*!" she replied.

It was my first trip outside of the United States, but I didn't have much time to enjoy Havana. My father was all business and at the first opportunity took us out of the city to visit tobacco plantations. He wanted me to learn firsthand how the world's finest tobacco was grown, selected, and packed.

I left Cuba with a new fascination for cigars and the deepest respect for the people who grew Havana tobacco, and I established lasting friendships with many of them. On our way back to Cleveland, I told my father the cigar business was definitely for me.

It was then that I discovered my cigar apprenticeship was far from over. Now my father informed me that he was sending me to Connecticut to learn how Connecticut tobacco was grown and sorted. He would not be accompanying me, as I was going to stay there for almost a year.

I had been to Connecticut before, having accompanied my father many times to buy wrapper tobacco. Ever since Cuban tobacco seeds were first planted in the Connecticut River Valley in the 1780s, Connecticut tobacco had been popular with cigar smokers around the world. Our company had been using Connecticut Broadleaf for binders and wrappers since the turn of the century.

It was during one of my first trips to Connecticut that I had learned one of the most important business lessons of my life. We were buying tobacco at a packing warehouse, and my father was letting me inspect the tobacco samples myself. There were about fifty leaves in each sample, and when I came to a good leaf, I pulled it out and showed it to him.

"See how good it looks!" I said.

When I came to a leaf that was off-color or broken, I put that aside. The owner was looking over our shoulders during all this—we had not yet come to a conclusion about the price—and my father said to him, "Excuse me, I want to tell Stanford something."

He took me outside and said, "Never do that again. When you look at tobacco, only point out the leaves that are poor. We're still negotiating the price. Every time you point out how good the tobacco looks, the price goes up. In business, you must remember to let the good things take care of themselves. It's the bad things you have to look out for."

Later, when I first started working in our cigar factory, this lesson was driven home once again. My father had asked me to walk through the factory and see how everything was going. When I completed my tour, he asked, "What did you see that was wrong?"

"Everything is right," I said.

"You go back and look again because you didn't look properly the first time. It is impossible to go through a factory of 400 employees and find that everything is perfect. There must be something wrong. There is no such thing as a business where everything is right."

To this day, whenever I evaluate something—be it a product, an advertisement, or a financial statement—I look for what is wrong with it. In business, you have to look at things critically, and spend your time correcting what is not right. As my father said, the good things will take care of themselves.

I arrived for my apprenticeship in Hartford, Connecticut, in September of 1938 with my suitcase in one hand and a portable typewriter in the other. My father expected me to send him weekly typewritten reports on my progress. At least it would help pass the time. There wasn't much to do in Hartford but work. I checked into the Milner Hotel, where a dollar a day got me room and board, and my laundry washed too.

When I showed up for work at the Hartman Tobacco Company, I was escorted into a warehouse staffed entirely by women. I was pretty good with the ladies on a one-on-one basis, but imagine being the only guy in a room full of 500 girls! I admit it was exciting, but it was also intimidating for a shy twenty-one-year-old guy like me. I got my fair share of teasing. The most fun I had was when the girls set up a phonograph in the cafeteria during lunch breaks and taught me the Charleston and other popular dances of the day.

Unfortunately, the warehouse was a pretty gruesome place. It was exceedingly cold and wet, and the water spray pipes that had been installed to keep the air humid constantly dripped on the backs of our necks. I had a cold the entire time I was in Hartford.

There wasn't much to do at the end of the day. The sun set so early in the winter that it was dark by the time I left the warehouse. Luckily, I discovered that the nearby Menninger Clinic employed a contingent of single nurses, who certainly helped the winter days pass more quickly.

Over the next eight months, I helped process tobacco, sort it by classification, and pack it. There were two kinds of tobacco that we worked with—Connecticut Broadleaf and Connecticut Shade. Broadleaf was grown in direct sunlight and was used as binder leaf or, when properly cured and fermented, for dark "maduro" wrappers. The other type was grown under a cloth canopy to protect it from sun and hail, hence the name: Shade. Its thin, delicate leaves were used exclusively for wrappers. We sorted the tobacco into a minimum of twenty different grades based on the quality and color of the leaf, separating leaves that were slightly torn or discolored from those in perfect condition, and ensuring that cigar manufacturers had the specific colors and textures they wanted. We then sorted the leaves by size, ranging from ten- to eighteen-inches long.

The Newfield and Hartman families, owners of Hartman Tobacco, grew their own Shade tobacco and purchased Broadleaf tobacco from small, independent farmers. I often rode with the Newfields' buyers on inspections of their small tobacco growers. These farmers ran no-frills operations, sorting Broadleaf tobacco in the basements of their farmhouses and scattering pots of boiling water on the floor to keep the air humid.

I also observed our competitors buying tobacco from the Newfields. Some of these executives were very good and knew what to look for. Others didn't have a clue. I dutifully reported all my observations to my father in my weekly typewritten reports.

I was overjoyed when March of 1939 arrived and I could go home. I returned to Cleveland armed with invaluable insights into the growing, processing, grading, inspecting, packing, and buying of tobacco.

Later that year, my friends and I rented a cottage on Lake Erie for a week. We were listening to the radio when the news came over that Germany had invaded Poland. We agreed that this was only the beginning, that Hitler would never stop. We saw it as only a matter of time before the United States would be forced to join the war effort.

As the war in Europe escalated over the next two years, I immersed myself in the cigar business. By now, my brother Millard had also joined the company. Our progress was interrupted when the Japanese attacked Pearl Harbor on December 7, 1941, and America entered World War II.

I felt it was my patriotic duty to defend my country. I had always been mechanically inclined, and believed the best use of my talents would be to serve in the Army Air Corps, which later became the Air Force. In January of 1942, two friends and I made a trip to Patterson Airbase in Dayton, Ohio, to enlist. Both of them were accepted into the aviation training program, but I was rejected after I failed a test for color blindness.

I immediately visited the draft board in Cleveland. They were very glad to see me. So many men in Cleveland had been exempted from service because they worked in the defense industry that the local board was short of their draft quotas. In April of 1942, I joined the Armed Forces. The only time in my life that I ever saw a tear in my father's eye was while saying our good-byes at the Cleveland train station.

As it turned out, I wound up in the Army Air Corps after all. The Air Corps was looking for 50,000 airplane mechanics at the time I joined, and all new recruits were being tested for mechanical aptitude. I passed the test with flying colors and, after six weeks of basic training

Ready to serve my country

in Biloxi, Mississippi, was sent to aviation engineering school in Ypsilanti, Michigan, where I was trained as a B-24 airplane specialist at a Ford aircraft plant.

The B-24 Liberator was a four-engine bomber and, with the B-17 Flying Fortress, played a major role in liberating the Allies from the Nazis. I believe more Liberators were built than any other bomber in U.S. history.

After six months training at the Ford plant, I was stationed at Topeka Army Airbase in Kansas as an engineer for a B-24 ground crew. The pilots and gunnery crews would stay there for six weeks of training before being sent overseas. I was one of the specialists who kept the engines running, working twenty-four hours on, twenty-four hours off.

Fellow Western Reserve grad Bob Dworkin and I enjoying a furlough during WWII

Toward the end of the war, the Air Corps was running out of qualified pilots, really scraping the bottom of the barrel. Some of these pilots simply couldn't fly the planes very well. Sometimes, they were so afraid of flying in the snow that they sabotaged the B-24s at night by idling the throttle and blowing some of the engine parts. I was the one who had to go outside in the freezing Kansas winter at three in the morning to repair them. Finally, I complained that the pilots were not only ruining the airplanes, they were ruining me. They cut it out pretty quickly. I'm afraid a few of them got court-martialed as a result of my whistle-blowing.

It was frustrating to be doing this kind of work when I knew I was qualified to do more. I was one of the only college graduates in our entire squadron of 1,500 men. I tried to apply for Officer's Candidate School, but my commanding officer wouldn't hear of it.

"I don't believe in ninety-day wonders, private!" he barked. "I went to West Point for four years! I will not allow soldiers like you who have only been in the Army for a short time to become officers in ninety days. That's no way to run the Army. After you've served two or three years, then you can apply for officer training."

One of the most challenging aspects of life in the service was sleeping in the Army barracks, where conditions were cramped, to say the least. Bunking with the other servicemen, stacked on top of each other like pancakes, felt like living in jail. I left the base every weekend that I possibly could. Naturally, all the other servicemen had the same idea, and finding a hotel room in Topeka on weekends was practically impossible. Being in the cigar business was helpful in this regard: I always managed to secure a reservation by bribing the desk clerk at my favorite hotel with cigars.

My days as an airplane engineer came to an end when I received a new classification as an office clerk. The only problem was that the job required typing, and I couldn't type. Luckily, the staff sergeant in charge of my department was a good friend of mine who arranged for me to take a typing class at a nearby high school. It was a little strange being the only man in uniform in a classroom filled with pimple-faced adolescents, but in any case, I accomplished my mission and learned how to type.

My new duties as an office clerk entailed processing Army transfer orders for the servicemen stationed at Topeka Airbase. One day, some paperwork crossed my desk indicating an opportunity to attend air traffic controller school at Fort Dix, New Jersey. I told my officer in charge that I wanted to go.

"You go ahead," he said. "Write your own orders."

I jumped at the chance to get out of Kansas, typed my own orders, and transferred to Fort Dix Army Airbase in the summer of 1944. After I arrived, I learned that you had to be classified in communications to attend air controller school. I lacked this qualification, but thankfully, was allowed to remain at Fort Dix.

In June of 1945, I returned to Cleveland for a few days to attend a once-in-a-lifetime event: the celebration of my father's fiftieth anniversary in the cigar business. I was amazed how many friends and business associates he had accumulated over the years. Many of them turned out for a testimonial gala at Cleveland's Hollenden Hotel. More than 180 executives had signed a scroll congratulating my father on his half-century in business. They had also commissioned an oil painting of him that hangs in our offices to this day. I hoped I would live to see the day we celebrated our hundredth anniversary.

GOLDEN ANNIVERSARY

1895 ★ 1945

M. & N. CIGAR MANUFACTURERS, INC. ★ CLEVELAND, OHIO

ASSOCIATES OF LONG STANDING

GEORGE KLEIN, 45 Years
EUGENE FRIED, 40 Years
EMIL LEDERER, 30 Years
BILL TEDOR, 25 Years
WILBUR HANTHORNE, 20 Years

1895 – 1945

BRANDS *that mean* BUSINESS

Four brands that millions of American smokers recognize for uniformly high quality.

STUDENT PRINCE

JUDGE WRIGHT

RIGOLETTO

JOHN CARVER

All famous products of

M & N CIGAR MANUFACTURERS, INC.
Cleveland, Ohio
Since 1895

A POST-WAR MESSAGE

Upon entering my fiftieth year in the cigar business, I believe that the post-war outlook for the industry is brighter than at any time since I can remember.

With Victory in sight, and with the coming return of our boys, demand for cigars will continue at its present pace. In fact, the war has undoubtedly made new cigar smokers from the ranks of the armed forces, and these boys will continue to want good cigars, in peace-time.

Retailers and jobbers who have been featuring STUDENT PRINCE Cigars will find that these products will continue to present outstanding values. The knowledge of 50 years experience assures dependability and quality of our products.

We thank you for your patience and your understanding of our problems in trying to meet the current demand. We will continue to do everything possible to assure a fair distribution of STUDENT PRINCE Cigars to our customers.

J.C. Newman
PRESIDENT

M & N CIGAR MANUFACTURERS, Inc.

Makers of STUDENT PRINCE Cigars

Like so many businesses during World War II, ours boomed, and Uncle Sam became our biggest customer. During the war, the Quartermaster Corps requisitioned forty percent of all the cigars we produced for shipment to servicemen overseas. We had to pack the cigars in huge wooden crates, which we waterproofed by lining them with tarpaper. Each crate had to be painted with color-coded stripes so if a transport ship were torpedoed and the crates floated in the sea, the military could easily tell what was inside and rescue more essential items like food and ammunition before saving the cigars.

The armed forces requisitioned so many of our cigars that we were forced to ration product to our regular, civilian customers. There was such a shortage that from 1942 to 1946 we had to limit each retailer to one box of cigars a week. Every time I came home on leave I would see our customers lined up outside our factory waiting to receive their weekly allotment. It was one of only two times in our history that we experienced a legitimate boom. More than half a century would pass before the next one came along. During this period, my father made a special point of taking good care of the William Edwards Company, who had given him his first substantial order back in 1895. He also raised about a million dollars selling war bonds through our company and brought three displaced European families to America, just as he had done during the First World War.

Back at Fort Dix, I was getting closer and closer to being assigned overseas as an air traffic controller. Before that happened, the war began to wind down. I was transferred to Fort Sumter, South Carolina, where I stayed until my discharge on December 15, 1945. I can't say I regret not going overseas. I was lucky I made it through the war unscathed. Many of my friends lost their lives. My two friends who had been accepted to train as pilots in the Air Corps were killed flying over Italy.

As I contemplated my impending return to the cigar industry, I decided that my first order of business would be to improve our tobacco blends. To do that, I would have to acquire a taste for cigars. It was time to become a cigar smoker. I wrote to my father and asked him to send me a box of fifty cigars. I intended to smoke all of them before returning to Cleveland.

Shortly thereafter, a box of Student Prince cigars arrived for me at Fort Dix. At the first opportunity, I settled down for my first smoke. I already had a good palate for food and wine.

I expected it would be easy to develop a taste for cigars. I soon discovered just how hard it could be. The cigars were so strong to me that I became extremely nauseated. It took me a full month smoking two cigars a day to become accustomed to them. By the time I finished the box of Student Prince, I was prepared to become a tobacco blender.

I had one final mission to accomplish before leaving the service. It was time to buy my own automobile. I had never owned one. Ever since I had taught myself to drive at the age of twelve, I had always been able to borrow someone's car. Now that I was a twenty-nine-year-old, soon to be ex-sergeant, I thought it was high time I acquired my own transportation. I bought a 1938 Chevy for $400 and sped out of South Carolina. My days in the military were over. I had done my patriotic duty and was ready to move on with my life.

Glad to be home: Millard and I with J.C. after returning to civilian life

When I returned to Cleveland on New Year's Day 1946, the first thing my mother asked me was if I had met any special girls during the war. I had dated a lot, but I never wanted to get married during my four years in the service. I actually had two or three opportunities to marry, but I believed it was irresponsible to start a family when I didn't know whether I would come out of the war dead or alive.

"Besides," I told my mother, "I haven't met anyone I really want to spend the rest of my life with. Of all the girls I've gone out with, not one of them had all the things I'm looking for. I'll probably never get married."

"Don't give up hope," she said. "You never know what the future may bring."

That afternoon, I received a phone call from my good friend Sandy Gins. We had been fraternity brothers at Western Reserve and Sandy had just returned from service as a lieutenant in the Navy. We hadn't seen each other in four years, so I told him to come on over.

Sandy showed up a few hours later with a girl on his arm. Her name was Elaine Weiner and she took my breath away. She was a knockout: statuesque, and beautiful enough to be a fashion model. (In fact, Elaine became a successful runway model just a few years later.) Her personality was equally disarming. This 22-year-old woman possessed a winning combination of feistiness, wit, and intelligence. I later found out that she was also a great cook, an important attribute as far as I was concerned.

Sandy and Elaine visited with me for about two hours. After they left, my mother and I exchanged looks.

"Do you still say you'll never get married?" she asked.

"Well, if I ever do marry, that is exactly the type of girl I want."

My mother just smiled at me.

I have always been the type of person who goes after what he wants. And at this point in my life, there was nothing I wanted more than to go out with Elaine. Still, I did not want to muscle in on my friend Sandy's territory. I refrained from calling Elaine until several months had passed, when I ran into Sandy at a nightclub and discovered he was seeing a different girl. Needing no further encouragement, I called Elaine the very next day.

Much to my dismay, I found out that the object of my affection was booked solid for the next five weeks. Elaine was probably the most eligible young woman in Cleveland, or at least it seemed that way to me. She was going out with someone new every single night. There had been very few young men around in Cleveland during the war. Elaine was making up for lost time now that the boys had come home. She penciled me in for a date five weeks hence.

Finally, the night of our first date arrived. We had a splendid time together. I turned on all my charms and managed to secure another date for the following Sunday. This was a major coup for me, as next Sunday was Easter, an important event on Cleveland's social calendar. Elaine could have had her pick of any number of eligible young men to escort her on Easter Sunday. I was very encouraged.

It was customary to give a corsage to your date on Easter. I resolved to give Elaine the most beautiful and extravagant corsage I could find. It cost me an arm and a leg, but I didn't care. She was surprised and delighted when I showed up on her doorstep with a corsage made of four orchids. We spent a wonderful Easter Sunday together strolling arm-in-arm through Wade Park, smiling and nodding to all the other couples dressed in their Sunday best. From that day on, Elaine dated no one but me.

Soon enough, it was time to introduce Elaine to my father. She was a little intimidated by him at first. The first thing he said to her was, "How tall you are, my dear." She had to stifle a laugh because she was only five-foot-six. That, of course, was tall for J.C. Newman.

Elaine made an effort to win my father over, giving him a big kiss on the cheek every time she met him. He wasn't used to such displays of affection—my mother never kissed him in public—and he absolutely loved it. Elaine later told me that my father was just a big softy if you knew how to get on his good side. I told her I had been trying to figure that one out for years.

Elaine and I were engaged in August of 1946. I wanted to get married the following year, after I had earned more money, but she had waited long enough to find a husband.

"You can get married next year if you want to, but I won't be around," she said. "I'm getting married this year!"

I was not about to lose her. We set a date of November 5, 1946.

While my fiancée busied herself with preparations for our wedding, I found myself drawn into a power struggle with my father's attorney for control of M & N. I had long suspected my father's lawyer cared more about advancing his own interests than about doing what was best for our company. When he called me into a surprise meeting with my father and brother, I discovered my suspicions were well founded.

"I am concerned about the future of M & N," the attorney began, addressing my father directly. "In the unfortunate event of your death, your sons will be unable to secure financing for the company. Stanford and Millard are too young. The banks won't loan money to the company under their leadership. They don't have the proper maturity and experience. I propose that your sons transfer their company stock into a trust fund administered by me. I will deal with the banks myself."

My father thought the arrangement was a wonderful idea. I was utterly opposed to it. This was nothing less than an attempted coup. Turning over my stock would be like handing him the company on a silver plate. I went straight to the president of our bank, the Union Bank of Commerce, to get his opinion on the matter.

"I'm glad you came to see me, Stanford," he said. "This attorney of yours has got it all backward. He says we won't loan M & N money if you and your brother are in charge? On the contrary, the reason we are loaning M & N money is *because* of you and your brother. We have every confidence in you. This attorney is trying to do something that is totally wrong for you and your future."

I explained all this to my father, but it took my mother's appeal to persuade him that the attorney's proposal was a bad idea. The attorney did not take the news well. "He'll be sorry!" he yelled. "Stanford's doing all the wrong things!"

It wasn't the last time that snake tried to take over our company. One day, he called the family into another meeting, saying that he wanted to tidy up my father's Will. I arrived early for the meeting so I'd have time to look over the new copy. He had replaced my name with his own as administrator of my father's estate.

"You tidied it up all right," I said. "You tidied it up for yourself!" We got out of there in a hurry.

After these unpleasant confrontations with my father's attorney, my upcoming honeymoon was shaping up to be just the escape I needed. Elaine and I wanted a small wedding, but my father demanded a big one. It was a grand affair with hundreds of guests and a fancy reception at the Alcazar Hotel in Cleveland Heights. My father surprised me with an extremely generous wedding present of a thousand dollars . . . or so I thought. Years later, after my father died, I discovered that he had borrowed the $1,000 from one of his own companies and recorded it as a loan to me. I was stuck repaying it.

Elaine and I, flanked by Gladys and J.C. on our wedding day

Gladys and Elaine make the social circuit together in 1949

Millard lends a hand at my wedding

Winning the most eligible young woman in Cleveland

Elaine proudly displays her new wedding ring while sitting with me during our honeymoon at the Astor Hotel

Without knowing the origin of our thousand dollars, Elaine and I skipped off to Bermuda for three weeks of uninterrupted bliss. Our honeymoon was the happiest time of my life thus far. It was her first time on an airplane. We stayed at the Eagle's Nest, the only hotel on the island that was accessible to civilians at the time. All the other hotels in Bermuda were still being allocated for military personnel.

We packed lunches and spent our days exploring the islands on rented bicycles. We dined and danced away the evenings with other newlyweds who were staying at the hotel. Everyone was in high spirits, not only because we were on honeymoon, but because we were still celebrating the end of the war.

On our way back to Cleveland, we made a stopover in New York City and stayed at the Hotel Astor on Times Square. It's no longer there, but in the 1940s, the Astor Bar was the hottest spot in town. There was even a song written about it. The lyrics were, "She had to go and lose it at the Astor!" We thought that was hysterical. Some of the newlyweds we had met in Bermuda were also visiting New York, and we all went out to Milton Berle's nightclub.

A well-earned day at the beach

Elaine does some wheeling and dealing of her own in Atlantic City

Finding a new home when we returned to Cleveland was a little tricky. There was a housing shortage just after the war and everything was rent-controlled by the Office of Price Stabilization. Eventually, we found a terrific duplex, a "side-by-side" they called it. The owner lived on one side and rented the other. He had served in the Armed Forces and wanted another veteran as his tenant.

After World War II, I became responsible for all manufacturing operations at M & N, while my brother, who had also just returned from service in the Air Corps, concentrated on sales. I was no longer interested in being a salesman. So much of a salesman's job is spent traveling and waiting to meet with customers. I hated sitting in waiting rooms thinking about the thousands of things I could accomplish if I were back at the factory.

My new responsibilities at M & N included purchasing cigar labels, and my first negotiation with Consolidated Lithograph in New York, one of our main label suppliers, turned out to be quite a learning experience. I was placing an order with their representative, Henry Topping, when he quoted a price he claimed was as low as he could go.

"Stanford, I'm offering these labels to you below cost," he said. "I'll lose money on this, but I'm willing to do it as a personal favor to you."

I was naïve enough to actually believe him. I felt so bad about it that I placed my next label order with a competing lithographer in Cincinnati, Ohio. I honestly thought I was doing Mr. Topping a favor.

When he called several months later to ask if I was ready to place my next order, I told him: "I have good news. I don't need any more labels from you. You said you were losing money on the deal so I found a new supplier."

He was flabbergasted.

"You thought you were doing me a favor?!" he scoffed. "Why didn't you give me a chance to meet the other guy's price? I could have sold them to you cheaper!"

His reaction took me by complete surprise.

"I thought you would be grateful," I stammered. "You told me you were losing money on us."

Mr. Topping was so distraught that he called our new supplier in Cincinnati and berated him for stealing one of his long-time customers. Never again was I so naïve.

Purchasing labels was a relatively minor duty compared to handling labor negotiations at the factory, another responsibility I assumed after the war. In January of 1948 I found myself involved in an especially tense labor negotiation with the union representing our factory workers: the IWW, short for International Workers of the World. Some people joked that what it really stood for was "I Won't Work."

After weeks of protracted negotiations, we had reached a stalemate over a five-cent difference between what our company was willing to pay and what the union would accept. It was midnight on a Saturday night and I was discussing the matter in private with our legal counsel, Karl Ertle, while the IWW representatives waited in the next room.

"I've decided to settle," I told Mr. Ertle. "We simply can't afford a strike right now."

We had just concluded an important contract with United States Tobacco Company to manufacture their Sano brand of denicotinized cigars. It was critical that we ship the order next week as promised; an interruption in operations was unthinkable. But Mr. Ertle was totally opposed to a settlement and told me so in no uncertain terms.

Home of M & N Cigar Manufacturers in 1945

"If you give in to the union now, you'll regret it for the rest of your life."

"I'll pay for your advice," I shot back, "but I don't have to take it."

He was extremely flustered by this and reluctantly agreed to settle. He didn't like it, but that's the way I wanted it.

We returned to the meeting and told the IWW we would give them the nickel increase. It turned out to be a wise decision. After the meeting adjourned, the union representatives told me they would have gone on strike first thing Monday morning had we not settled with them that very evening.

Fortunately, my job included other, more enjoyable, activities. During the 1948 Cleveland Indians baseball season (so far the last time the Indians won the World Series), I was involved in a promotion whereby every Cleveland Indian hitting a home run received a free box of Student Prince cigars. After one game, I arranged to have a photograph taken of me presenting cigars to that evening's two home run hitters, Larry Doby, the first African-American to play in the American League, and Al Rosen, who later became president of the

San Francisco Giants. The next day, I received a frantic phone call from the vice president of the Indians requesting that the roll of film be destroyed. He explained that, by contract, players in uniform were prohibited from promoting and publicizing any tobacco products. The photographs were never published, although I held onto the negatives for myself.

Two of my most important accomplishments after I returned from the war involved making changes to both our tobacco blending and accounting departments. Not having smoked cigars until very recently turned out to be an advantage in terms of improving our tobacco blends. I had what you might call a virgin palate for tobacco and was keenly aware of nuances in taste.

My top priority was to give our cigars more character. Our tobacco blenders in the factory kept telling me people wanted mild cigars, but I believed that if you made something too mild, customers might well claim to enjoy it on a first try, but there was nothing about it to make them want to smoke it again. People only think they want a mild cigar. They don't. What they really want is something with more taste and aroma, something memorable. The most successful restaurants do not serve bland food. I saw myself as a chef cooking up delicious blends of tobacco. I called upon all the knowledge I had gained from my time in Connecticut and Cuba and, relying on my own sense of taste, worked hard to improve our blends.

Updating our accounting procedures was equally important. Our company accountants were all right, but they didn't know much about cost accounting for the cigar business. They just recorded how much money we took in, subtracted what we spent on merchandise, and what was left was profit. But it's not that simple, especially when you want to profitably launch a new product.

I worked out a standard costing system that took into account all of our variable and fixed expenses so that we could tell on a weekly basis how much profit and loss we were making on a given product. That was so important, because if we saw a problem—say our tobacco yield was down—we could do something about it immediately, rather than waiting two or three months, when it might be too late to correct a problem. In time, I put a system in place that made a huge difference in our ability to respond quickly to the changing cigar market. We still use the same system today.

With all my new responsibilities, you would think my father might have offered me a raise. Not so. I had to ask him to increase my salary from $85 a week to $100 a week just to meet

Presenting boxes of Student Prince to home run hitters Al Rosen
. . . and Larry Doby

my personal expenses. He refused at first, claiming it wouldn't look good to the other employees if he paid me more. Only after I asked my mother to intercede did he finally comply.

Just as I was getting settled back in business after the war, we received some troubling news from the Quartermaster Corps. It seemed that they had a large quantity of cigars they wished to return to us. In fact, they wanted us to buy back millions of cigars they had stockpiled from as early as 1942. The cigars were now so old and dried out as to be unsaleable.

My father refused to accept these ruined cigars.

"I will not pay for the government's mistake!" he railed. "It's all their fault for not handling them properly. Now they want me to take them back at full price? Out of the question."

The Quartermaster Corps politely indicated they would find someone else to buy them.

Shortly thereafter, one of our distributors returned some dried-out cigars to us, claiming to have purchased them from M & N. Upon further investigation we discovered that the government had in fact originally purchased these cigars back in the early 1940s. To our horror, we soon learned that the Quartermaster Corps had been selling our cigars to professional liquidators at huge discounts of twenty cents on the dollar. These liquidators then made a killing by selling the cigars to tobacco distributors for fifty cents on the dollar. Completing this vicious circle, our distributors now came calling on us in droves, demanding full credit for these useless cigars.

We immediately saw the potential for disaster. If distributors started dumping these old cigars on the market, the reputation of our brands would be ruined. We had no choice but to buy back all our cigars directly from the Quartermaster Corps—hundreds of thousands of them, and at full price.

By early 1947 we were destroying more cigars than we were manufacturing. It was a disaster of epic proportions, not only for us, but for all American cigar manufacturers, who suffered a similar fate. After enjoying such a boom during the war, we were now forced to cut our day shift in half and completely eliminate our night shift. In addition, my father was considering a ten percent pay cut for all of our employees. I objected to this.

"If we're going to stay in business," I said, "people working for us shouldn't have their pay cut. We have to find some other way to get through this."

My father had survived a great many catastrophes, but this one had him absolutely stumped. All his life he had known what to do. He had looked to me only to follow orders. For the first time, he truly needed my help. He came to me with his head in his hands.

"What are we going to do, son?"

THE FATAL PENNY

e've got to get this factory going again."
This was my advice to my father and
my call to action for the company.

At the height of the War Boom in 1945 we had moved into our biggest factory yet, a former defense plant. Now this gigantic factory was running at barely half its capacity. To turn
our company around, we had to get the factory up to speed. The question was: What type of
cigars should we manufacture?

When cigars became scarce during the war, prices had increased, in most cases without
a corresponding increase in the size of the cigars. As most cigars were now selling for ten
cents, I felt our first order of business should be to develop a cigar that made smokers feel
they were getting their ten cents' worth. My father agreed, and we came out with an extra
thick ten-cent cigar called Student Prince General in a size and shape that was different from
anything else on the market. It sold extremely well, but it was only a temporary solution to
a larger problem.

My father had been steering us in the direction of higher-quality, higher-priced cigars
for some time. One of his favorite sayings was: "If you make and sell something on the
basis of quality, you can stay in business for a hundred years. If you make and sell something on the basis of price, someone can always make it cheaper, and you'll be out of business in six months." I actually agreed with his philosophy, but at the time I felt the only
way we could get out of our slump was by competing more effectively in the lower-priced
segment.

My father objected to this strategy. "I don't want to make cheap cigars!"

"Well, here's the alternative," I countered. "We either make low-priced cigars or we go
out of business!"

I believed we could make a better five-cent cigar than anyone else in the industry. My
new cost accounting system allowed us to monitor and control our expenses more accurately

than before, which helped us bring out new products under tighter margins. Furthermore, I believed my skills as a blender were such that I could come up with a less expensive tobacco blend that still offered better taste and aroma than our competitors' five-cent cigars.

"But how?" my father asked. "Where can we get wrappers?"

That was a difficult question. We could get away with using lower-priced tobacco for filler and binder, but high-quality wrapper was essential. And to our great frustration, some of the larger cigar manufacturers had artificially driven up the price of Connecticut wrapper tobacco in a conspiracy to drive smaller companies like ours out of business.

This is how it worked. The big northern cigar companies grew most of their wrapper tobacco themselves, buying only ten percent on the open market. Thus, they could afford to offer ridiculously high prices to their outside suppliers of Connecticut Shade wrapper because they could average the price down against the cheaper tobacco they grew themselves. We had no such luxury. Independent firms like M & N were too small to grow our own tobacco. Our only hope was to find a new source of wrappers.

Not to be discouraged, I made a few phone calls, bought a couple of train tickets, and took my father to visit some tobacco dealers in the town of Quincy, Florida, the center of Florida Shade wrapper tobacco production. We both could see that Florida wrapper was not of the exact same quality as Connecticut Shade, but it was far more affordable and, in my opinion, more than adequate. My father was reluctant. I told him that combining Florida Shade wrapper with Pennsylvania filler and Connecticut Broadleaf binder would produce a better blend than any other five-cent cigar on the market. He decided to trust me and we returned to Cleveland having purchased several hundred bales of Florida wrappers.

Rather than introducing my new nickel cigar as an entirely new brand (never a good idea in the cigar business), I made it an extension of the Cameo brand that had saved my father's business during the Depression.

I had been correct in my assumptions: There was indeed a pent-up demand for a better quality five-cent cigar, and my new Cameo Bouquet was an instant success. Distributors started placing repeat orders for 100,000 and 200,000 at a time. Cameo Bouquet was soon selling at a rate of more than sixty million cigars a year. Our factory returned to wartime levels of production and our company returned to profitability.

Our biggest distributor at the time was a company in Kansas City called Niles and Moser. They had a hundred salesmen who sold nothing but cigars in seventeen states throughout the

The cast of "The Student Prince" and I toast to the operetta with the cigar of the same name

Midwest. My father and I visited the owner, Ray Niles, toward the end of 1948. He was very happy with his Cameo Bouquet sales. We didn't know just how happy until we settled down for our meeting.

"Five-cent cigars are doing very well right now," he began. "We're selling a couple of different brands, but we can barely keep up with the demand. We're looking for a very special brand to feature as our leading nickel cigar. I'm very impressed with Cameo Bouquet; I think the quality is better than anything else on the market. Can you supply us with, say, a million a week?"

I was ecstatic about his offer. It was a vindication of all my hard work on Cameo Bouquet.

I left the meeting for a few minutes to check in with the office. While I was out of the room, without ever having discussed it with me, my father casually told Mr. Niles, "By the way, on Monday we're increasing the price of Cameo Bouquet to six cents. I trust that won't be a problem."

I returned to the meeting ignorant of what my father had done. As I entered his office, I was stunned to hear Ray Niles rescinding his offer.

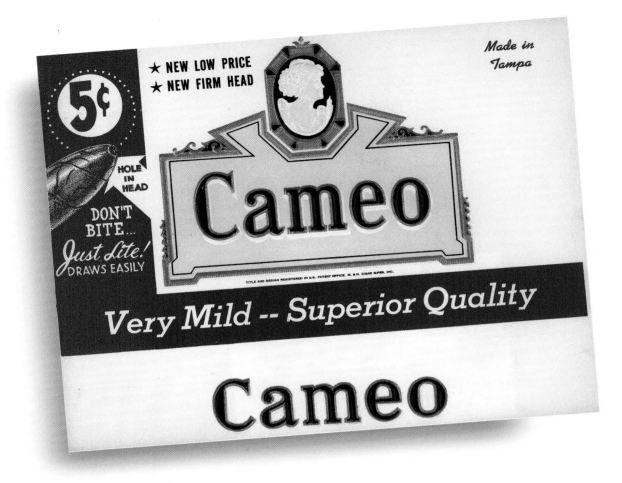

"It's very disappointing to hear you say that, J.C.," he was saying. "I'm not looking for a six-cent cigar. I'll have to find someone else to give me my million a week."

I could have told my father that Ray Niles would react this way! Cigars were stuck at fixed prices of five, ten, fifteen cents, and two for a quarter. The public accepted these categories as sacred. Consumers were willing to pay more for other goods after the war, but they had it in their heads that they were not going to pay more for tobacco products. People would drive an extra mile, spend extra money on gas, just to save a penny on a cigar. This was largely because smokers were accustomed to paying very little for cigarettes, which were marketed as loss leaders and sold below cost to get customers into the stores.

Some of our competitors tried moving outside these rigid price brackets. Consolidated Cigar raised their Dutch Masters and El Producto from two for a quarter to two for twenty-seven cents. Consumers wouldn't buy it and Consolidated eventually rescinded the increase.

My father had tried the same thing with our Student Prince President, raising the price from ten cents to eleven, with the same result. Who wanted to pay eleven cents for a cigar they were accustomed to getting for a dime?

We walked out of Ray Niles's office and I pulled my father aside. I was appalled.

"What did you say that for?"

"Oh, Stanford, calm down. It's only a penny. It won't make any difference. If people like them at five cents, they'll like them at six. I don't want to produce a million cigars a week without making a profit."

True to his word, Ray Niles found another manufacturer to give him a million five-cent cigars a week. Our six-center couldn't compete. The consequences of that fatal penny were devastating. We lost half our Cameo Bouquet business overnight.

We had lost a major battle, but there was still a war to be won. The economic boom following World War II had completely changed the marketplace. Americans were making more money and traveling more frequently. Consumers wanted to find the same brands wherever they traveled. Local and regional brands were no longer viable. National brands were the name of the game. We had to start playing by the new rules.

Before World War II, there were at least 300 local breweries across the United States. After the war, the breweries began to close. They couldn't compete with national brands like Miller or Budweiser. It was the same thing with cigars. We would be stupid not to adjust to this trend and make our brands available on a national basis.

My father was skeptical about a national expansion. Many cigar manufacturers had been burned trying to create national brands. The most famous failed attempt to market a national cigar brand involved a strange promotion called the Anti-Spit Campaign.

I discovered the use of spit in cigar making during one of my first visits to my father's cigar factory when I was ten years old. I was watching one of the cigarmakers rolling a cigar when I saw her stick the end in her mouth and use her saliva to seal the head and keep the cigar from unraveling. I looked around and realized that all the cigarmakers—some 400 women on the factory floor—were doing the same thing.

"That's disgusting!" I exclaimed to our factory foreman, Mr. Landesman. "Why do they *do* that?"

"To get the wrapper to stay down right, you have to wet it a little before you close it up."

"But why don't they use water or something? Do they have to use spit?"

"These women are paid by the number of cigars they make each week. Piecework, we call it. To make the most money, they have to work as fast as they can. It's quicker to stick a cigar in your mouth than it is to use the vegetable gum we provide to each cigarmaker. We're not the only cigar company that does this, Stanford. It's common practice."

"But this is terrible!" I protested. "Now I can't bring any of my friends to see the factory. What would they think if they saw everybody sticking the cigars in their mouths?"

"Oh, don't worry. We have it all worked out."

Just then, a group of visitors came onto the factory floor.

"Watch this," he said.

Mr. Landesman raised his arm and immediately everyone on the floor stopped licking the cigars and began using the vegetable gum.

"When I stick up my arm, that's a secret signal to everyone to stop using spit," he whispered conspiratorially. As soon as the visitors left, the cigars went back in everyone's mouths.

My father never knew spit was being used on his cigars. He would have been mortified had he found out: J.C. Newman took great pride in operating a "sanitary cigar factory," even boasting of this in his advertisements.

Higher powers than I recognized the revulsion smokers would feel if they knew spit was commonly used to make cigars. In fact, one manufacturer tried to exploit the situation to his advantage.

In 1929, my father and I were visiting a distributor in Chicago when we happened to strike up a conversation with a sales manager from American Cigar Company, a subsidiary of American Tobacco Company, the one-time cigarette monopoly that Teddy Roosevelt had busted up in 1911. This sales manager was very excited.

"Have you seen our Anti-Spit Campaign?" he asked.

Indeed we had. Everyone in the cigar industry had seen the huge billboards trumpeting Cremo as "The Sanitary Cigar." George Washington Hill, the president of American Tobacco, had decided to sell his Cremo cigar brand on a national basis, like cigarettes. This was highly

THE MODERN SANITARY CIGAR FACTORY

The Sanitary Cigar Factory—if my father had only known!

unusual in 1929. Most cigars were still made by hand and sold regionally, but American Tobacco had installed cigar machines in some of its factories to churn out Cremo cigars.

"We're advertising the fact that Cremo doesn't use spit," the sales manager continued. "Our ads say, 'Wouldn't you be horrified if you suddenly discovered that the cigar you smoked was tipped with spit? Smoke Certified Cremo and protect yourself against this abomination!' It's all part of a big promotion to make Cremo a national cigar brand. We're giving a car away every day to customers who send in the most Cremo cigar bands. I've got five hundred salesmen on it."

Before he could say anything more he was interrupted by a phone call. He excused himself and was gone for about ten minutes. When he returned, the enthusiastic sales manager was gone. In his place was a man who looked as if the sky had fallen.

"I was just told to fire my five hundred salesmen. Cremo is not selling fast enough for George Washington Hill. He decided he doesn't want to spend any more money promoting Cremo cigars."

In New York Spit is a horrid word, but it is worse on the end of your cigar

... the war against Spitting is a crusade of decency ... join it. Smoke CERTIFIED CREMO!

Hating "spit" as you do, wouldn't you be horrified if you suddenly discovered that the cigar you smoked was rolled by filthy fingers—and tipped with spit?

Why take chances? Smoke **Certified Cremo** and protect yourself against this abomination! Every tobacco leaf entering the clean, sunny **Certified Cremo** factories is scientifically treated by methods developed by the United States Government during the war. And its purity is safeguarded along every step of the way by amazing inventions that foil, wrap and tip the cigars without the possibility of spit!

Try a **Certified Cremo**—see how wonderfully good it is! Made of the choicest, tenderest leaves that the crop affords, we claim **Certified Cremo's** quality is tastier than that of any other cigar. Don't let its 5c price stand in your way. **Certified Cremo** is the kind of cigar your physician has in mind when he recommends a mild smoke in place of heavy brands.

Crush-proof ... immaculate ... foil-wrapped ... **Certified Cremo** is the kind of cigar the late Vice-President Marshall undoubtedly had in mind when he said, "What this country needs is a good 5c cigar!"

Certified
Cremo
THE GOOD 5¢ CIGAR
...THAT AMERICA NEEDED

© 1930 American Cigar Co.

Certified **Cremo** Sanitary and Clean

Cremo's famous Anti-Spit campaign

That was the end of American Tobacco's experiment in mass-market cigars for the time being. The timing just wasn't right for a national cigar brand. Regional brands were still too strong.

Almost twenty years later, the timing couldn't be better. Regional cigar brands were going the way of the dinosaur. Our future depended upon making the transition from a regional to a national cigar company. Otherwise, we would die on the vine. First, I had to convince my father.

"Most cigars have been regional brands, that's true," I started. "But no more. People are traveling extensively these days. They want the same brand of cigar whether they're in Cleveland or California. We have to figure out how to go national. If we don't, we might as well sell our business to somebody else!"

That always grabbed my father's attention. He agreed to give it a try. But how were we going to do it? Expanding beyond the ten Midwestern states in which we were already operating was very, very difficult.

We started in Detroit and called on the best distributor in town, the prestigious John T. Woodhouse Cigar Company. Mr. Woodhouse already had brands that were selling, and was afraid his current cigar suppliers would threaten him: "If you take on a competing brand from another manufacturer, we'll take our brand away from you." Mr. Woodhouse told us he would only take our brands if they were already established in his market! It seemed like a no-win situation, but he actually gave us a clue as to how we could break into new markets.

We only had one shot at this. If we got in with the wrong distributor and our brands didn't sell, we'd probably never get a second chance in that market. When we couldn't get the top distributor in a given market, we would not go after number two or three. Instead, we would either pass on that market and come back to it later or, thanks to Mr. Woodhouse's suggestion, set up our own distribution network.

We leased a warehouse, hired our own salesmen, and opened our first distribution center in Detroit. My brother-in-law, Al Rogan, became our Michigan branch sales manager. He promoted our cigars in local newspapers and sponsored radio news reports and weather forecasts. Within a year, he had made Rigoletto, Student Prince, and Cameo some of the leading brands in the state. It was time to go back to Mr. Woodhouse.

This time, we told him exactly what he wanted to hear.

"We want to get out of the distribution business," we told him. "We're proud of what we've done with our brands in this market, but we're manufacturers, not distributors. That's your area. We've got a lot of business here in Michigan and we'd like to give it all to you."

The deal was done. We closed our Michigan branch office knowing that our brands were in the best possible hands.

My brother Millard, our sales manager, went to California, a critical territory for any business hoping to go national. We tried to duplicate what worked for us in Michigan and set up our own distribution system, but California was too far from Cleveland. From the time our salesmen delivered our product, to the time we generated an invoice out of Cleveland, it took far too long for us to get paid by our customers.

It was imperative that we find a distributor. Millard looked no further than Marcus Glaser, whose company, Glaser Brothers Tobacco Distributors, practically owned California. Glaser had little interest in our brands. But Millard was one of the best salesmen I have ever known and this job required all his powers of persuasion. He kept after Glaser until finally, in exasperation, Glaser half-jokingly told Millard he would reconsider if Millard convinced Thrifty Drug, one of California's leading drug store chains, to buy cigars through Glaser instead of directly from M & N.

Thrifty Drug had a long-standing policy of buying cigars directly from manufacturers. They shunned middleman tobacco distributors like the plague. Glaser never dreamed he would have to make good on his promise. But Millard had a golden tongue and managed to convince Thrifty Drug to make an exception. Glaser won the right to distribute M & N brands to Thrifty Drug and in return, promoted our brands throughout his own statewide distribution channels.

New York City was an easier nut to crack. There were so many big cigar retailers in the city that we had no need for a distributor. We were lucky to be headquartered in "the best location in the nation," as Cleveland was sometimes called. More than half the population of the United States is within five hundred miles of Cleveland, which means that major eastern cities like New York are within a day's truck ride for the delivery of goods. We employed eight salesmen in the New York City area and shipped cigars directly from our factory in Cleveland. There were so many cigar stores in New York that some of our salesmen could spend an entire day making sales calls on a single city block.

Despite my father's blunder with Cameo Bouquet, Ray Niles gave us our most significant entrée into the national arena. My father had been friendly with Ray since the Depression and he had gone out of his way to supply Niles and Moser with cigars during the worst shortages of World War II. Ray Niles now repaid my father's loyalty a hundredfold by agreeing to distribute our Student Prince General cigars in the seventeen Midwestern states he serviced. The fatal penny was forgiven.

Ray Niles's example led the way for other major distributors throughout the country to open their doors to us. We were well on our way to becoming a national cigar company.

LIGHTNING CAPITAL OF THE WORLD

CHAPTER 5

As my father advanced into his late seventies, any illusions I had about his mellowing with age were quickly dispelled. If anything, J.C. became even more outspoken about how things should be done. He was especially vocal about his dream of taking our company out of the cheap cigar business and into the more prestigious high-quality, high-priced premium cigar market.

We had begun using more Cuban tobacco, which certainly enhanced our reputation for quality, and had the added benefit of being more affordable than the still-overpriced Connecticut Shade. Unfortunately, by the time our Cuban tobacco arrived in Cleveland, it wasn't always the same tobacco it had been in Cuba; it tended to lose some of its distinct aroma in the freezing temperatures on the trip north.

In the spring of 1953, I received an urgent telephone call from my father. He claimed to have found a possible solution to our problem.

"Stanford, it's time for a radical change," he began. This was one of my father's favorite rallying cries in his later years. I braced myself.

"I'm down in Tampa, Florida, visiting Bunny Annis," he said.

Bunny, whose real first name was Julius, like my father's, was an old friend of the family. He was also a fellow cigar manufacturer. His company, Gradiaz Annis, made Gold Label, one of the most popular Tampa cigar brands at that time. My father had stopped by for a visit on his way home from a tobacco-buying excursion in Cuba.

"I just saw an empty cigar factory that's perfect for us," he said, his excitement palpable. "I want you to fly down to Tampa immediately and take a look at it. I think I'm going to buy it."

One of my father's lifelong hobbies was looking at old buildings and imagining how they could be converted into cigar factories. He'd moved our company into quite a few of them over the years. In my opinion, he had sometimes gone overboard, needlessly overextending the company's finances in his reckless acquisition of one factory building after another. Now, at seventy-eight, when most people his age had long since retired, he was seriously considering buying this building in Tampa and moving our entire operation to Florida.

In some ways, my father's idea made sense. Tampa's high-priced premium cigar market was one of the few segments in the cigar industry that had actually grown in sales and profitability after the Second World War. In fact, since the turn of the century, more hand-rolled Clear Havana cigars—cigars made entirely of Cuban tobacco—had been made in Tampa than in Cuba itself. It was the perfect place to establish a reputation for quality. And Tampa's climate was perfect for cigar making; there would be no problems with frozen tobacco here. The heat and humidity were ideal for keeping tobacco in a pliable condition.

On the other hand, the Tampa cigar industry had not adapted well to the machine age. Tampa cigars were justly famous for their quality—getting the "Made in Tampa" association was what appealed to my father—but machine-made cigars had dominated the industry ever since the Depression and Tampa had failed to change with the times. Cigarmakers' unions were so entrenched in Tampa that it had been difficult for Tampa's cigar manufacturers to make the conversion from handmade to machine-made cigars.

Strikes had been a Tampa tradition since Cuban cigarmakers migrated there in the 1880s, having first settled in Key West at the outbreak of Cuba's Civil War in 1868. Tampa cigarmakers even referenced personal milestones like marriages and the births of their children in relation to major strikes, which occurred regularly with each new decade.

Union leaders were historically antagonistic to employers. It was considered taboo to get too friendly with management. The union also exerted undue control over the prices cigarmakers were paid. They resisted employer policies whenever possible, even demanding extra pay to re-roll cigars they had made poorly. The very cigar factory my father wanted to buy was available only because its owner had closed and moved his business to Pennsylvania because of difficulties with the union.

In Cleveland, I was well experienced with the difficulties involved in running a union cigar factory. My introduction to the unions occurred in 1938, just before I joined M & N full-time. We were making machine-made cigars out of Connecticut Broadleaf, which is not easy to work with. It stains your hands more than other kinds of tobacco when it's wet, and the cigarmakers had to stop frequently to clean their machines. It was a demanding job, but rather than trying to find a way to improve the situation, the cigarmakers threw up their hands and walked out. They refused to return to the factory until we gave them the kind of tobacco they wanted to work.

At that point, we were not a union cigar factory. One of the cigarmakers was married to a union agent who brought union representatives into our factory. They distributed leaflets to our employees depicting my father swinging a baseball bat studded with spikes over their heads! Our factory was unionized in short order. After that, whenever they didn't like something, they simply sat down on the factory floor and stopped work. How could we possibly compete in Tampa, where the unions were even more restrictive?

I flew down to Tampa to see if there was a possibility of being successful.

Arriving in Tampa, the first thing that struck me was the heat: unbearable for a Northern guy from Ohio. It was all well and good for my father to spend the remainder of his years in the warm Florida climate; I was the one who would have to raise my family and run the business here after he was gone. I've long since come to love Tampa, but at the time I didn't like it one bit.

The next thing that struck me was the sheer number of cigar factories in the city. Tampa had once been the largest cigar-manufacturing center in the world. Sixty cigar factories had been built there between 1886 and 1910, and all of them were designed the same way: three stories high and fifty feet across. Every factory ran east to west, with the broadest side of the building facing north.

In the days before electric lights, a northern exposure was essential to the task of sorting tobacco leaves, which were traditionally sorted into as many as fifty different shades of color. Direct sunlight from the east or west made it extremely difficult to ascertain the true color of the tobacco leaves. Indirect northern light was ideal. In the early days of the Tampa cigar industry, tobacco sorters were sent home on cloudy days.

The factory I had come to see was located in Ybor City, a historic cigar-making district founded in 1886 by a famous Cuban revolutionary named Vincent Ybor. The Regensburg Company, makers of a popular cigar brand named Admiration, had built the factory in 1910. It was one of the last—and largest—cigar factories ever built in Tampa.

El Reloj, a Tampa landmark (1910)

Every cigar factory in Tampa had a nickname. The Regensburg factory was nicknamed El Reloj, Spanish for clock, because of its handsome red brick clock tower. El Reloj was a Tampa landmark. For decades, local residents had risen in the morning and gone to bed at night according to the hourly chimes of the Regensburg clock tower.

My father was impressed with the history and size of the factory. His heart was set on buying it and there was nothing I could do to dissuade him. So I made a deal with him.

"Let's try this in a small way," I said. "Why don't we lease one floor of the factory to start. I'll send down ten machines, hire enough people to operate them, and get it going. After one year, if it looks like we can succeed here, we'll move our entire operation down from Cleveland. If things don't work out, we'll return our machines to Cleveland and close our Tampa operation."

Just as when I first approached my father about becoming M & N's downtown salesman in 1935, I had one make-or-break condition for taking on this responsibility.

"You have to let me do all the hiring. I want to interview everyone myself and make all the decisions about who we hire."

My father conceded and I returned to Cleveland to break the news to my wife. Elaine wasn't too happy to hear we might be moving to Tampa. I told her we wouldn't know for sure until we saw the results of our trial operation.

The union at our Cleveland factory was already making noises about yet another contract negotiation. I was in charge of working with them and resolved to hold off on finalizing a new contract until we saw how things played out in Tampa.

Meanwhile, my father and I set up a subsidiary of M & N for our Tampa operation named Standard Cigar Company. In June of 1953, I returned to Tampa to get the operation started. I had never opened a cigar factory before, but I was determined to be successful.

At first I couldn't even get inside the factory because there was so much junk piled up against the door. I walked across the street to a drug store called La Economica and looked in a telephone book for industrial cleaning companies. I found one and asked them to send a cleaning crew over immediately.

Once the factory was cleaned up, I consulted someone I knew in Tampa's leaf tobacco business named Tony Muniz, who helped me arrange to hire a few key employees, including an experienced bookkeeper and a person who had experience in moistening, or "casing," tobacco. I went back to Cleveland and arranged for ten cigar machines to be shipped to Tampa.

When I returned to Tampa at the end of June, I was shocked to find hundreds of people waiting for me on the steps of our factory. Unbeknownst to me, the mechanics that set up our cigar machines had spread the word that a new cigar company was coming to town. Now I had to contend with a huge crowd of unemployed cigarmakers looking for work. Most of them were former employees of the Regensburg factory, which had once employed 1,500 people. I passed out hundreds of applications and told the assembled crowd that I would start interviewing in a day or two.

Three hundred people showed up the morning of my first day of interviews. Five hundred more showed up that afternoon. Just about every person I interviewed appeared to be fifty or older. I'm sure many of them were in their eighties. Almost none of them had ever operated a cigar machine. Without exception, they were all union cigarmakers.

I went back to my hotel at the end of the day feeling discouraged. My wife had come to Tampa with me, and I shared my concerns with her over dinner that night.

"This is not going to work," I said. "These people have been making cigars by hand for decades. We'll never be able to train them to operate cigar machines. Furthermore, they're all union cigarmakers. I have nothing against the unions. If I worked under some of the conditions these people have had to deal with, I would want a union too. But the union has far too much control over manufacturing operations. If they get started in our factory, I'll never be able to run things my way. I've heard rumors that, in the thirties, these cigarmakers had to leave a dollar on their cigar tables every Friday to be split between the union bosses and the factory supervisors. If they didn't leave the dollar, they didn't come back to work on Monday, or any day. Where am I going to find suitable workers for the factory?"

Elaine thought a walk outside might do us both some good. As we strolled through downtown Tampa past the offices of the local newspaper, I realized that the solution to my problem might be remarkably simple.

I immediately went inside the Tampa Tribune building and placed a classified ad: "Female help wanted—no experience required—excellent opportunity for advancement." To keep the union out and ensure that none of my employees were preconditioned to antiquated cigar-making practices, I resolved to hire only young people who had no experience making cigars. I familiarized myself with a map of Greater Tampa and when the first responses to my ad came in, I only hired those who lived outside the City of Tampa, figuring they would be far less likely to know anything about cigars.

Within ten days of placing my first classified, I had hired my first fifteen employees. After they were hired, I told all of them, "If it's going to bother you to work in a place where there's no union, please don't work here." I went on to explain that while we did not want a union in our factory, we would pay our employees at least as much if not more than the union factories paid.

We brought a mechanic and an instructor down from Cleveland to train our new learners on the cigar machines, and hired a man named Jerry LaPrell, who soon became one of our most valued employees, as treasurer and office manager. On July 5, 1953, Standard Cigar Company was up and running in the City of Tampa.

For the next twenty-five years, I conducted interviews every Monday morning and personally hired everyone who came to work for us. One of my pet peeves in building a business is that the responsibility for hiring is often given to lower-level employees. Finding good people is one of the most important things there is, yet many companies have someone whom they ordinarily wouldn't trust to buy paper clips interviewing people. I believe interviewing is a responsibility that belongs with senior management. I have interviewed thousands of people over the years and never regretted the investment of my time.

Standard Cigar Company, 1953

One afternoon shortly after I opened our factory I received an unexpected visit from a local businessman who wished to discuss a proposition. I had no idea what sort of business he was in and I was very busy at the time. I told him I could spare only a few minutes. He promised it wouldn't take long.

"I would like to offer you $150 a week for the exclusive right to operate bolita concessions in your factory," he said.

"What's bolita?" I asked. I had no idea.

"If you haven't seen bolita yet, you will soon enough. Bolita is very popular in Tampa. It's a lottery game. Most people here play it, and all the cigar factories have bolita concessions."

"I'll think about it," I said.

I prefer not to say no to anyone until I have had time to think things over. He agreed to return a week later for my decision.

That week I did a little investigating. While walking the streets of Ybor City, I came across a bolita game in progress. I noticed a huge crowd gathered outside one of the cigar factories and wandered over to see what was going on. I saw a bag of what looked like golf balls being tossed into the cheering crowd. Someone caught it, opened the bag, and pulled out several bolita balls at random, reading out numbers inscribed on the balls. Everyone in the crowd consulted the numbered bolita tickets they had purchased. The person whose ticket numbers matched the sequence of numbers read out from the balls was declared the winner.

Now that I understood how bolita was played, I asked around to find out the inside story. It was rumored that many bolita games were fixed. The organizers of the game would secretly prepare a few bolita balls ahead of time, putting them on ice before placing them in the bag with the other, room-temperature balls. The bag was then thrown to one of the organizers' cronies standing in the crowd. He pulled out only the cold balls and read off the numbers in ascending or descending order, as agreed upon in advance. The numbers corresponded exactly to the tickets held by one of the organizers' buddies.

When the bolita man came back to see me, I made it clear that I wanted nothing to do with this numbers game.

"Perhaps you do not understand," he said. "Bolita is played in every cigar factory in Tampa. Your workers will expect it."

"Our employees can play bolita on their own time if they want to, but not here. I don't want any gambling going on in our factory. The answer is no."

The bolita man left in a huff.

A day or two later, another local businessman came to see me at the factory. I told him right away that if he had come to talk about bolita, he was wasting his time.

"Nothing like that," he said. "I am a vendor of Cuban coffee. I have an arrangement with many of the cigar manufacturers here in Tampa to sell coffee in their factories. I will give you $100 a week for the right to be your exclusive coffee concession."

"I'll get back to you," I said.

Once again, I investigated. I learned that drinking Cuban coffee in the cigar factories was as much of a Latin tradition in Tampa as playing bolita. Cigarmakers worked with a coffee cup by their side. Coffee vendors would pass through the factory several times a day, refilling the cigarmakers' cups for three cents.

In Cleveland, we had no such custom. Furthermore, I didn't like the idea of coffee spilling onto our cigar machines. Having outsiders bringing coffee into our factory also made me uncomfortable. Finally, our Tampa employees had no previous experience in the cigar industry and therefore, would not expect a coffee concession. I said no.

Two kickback offers in one week! Had I accepted them, I could have doubled my income. In my book, however, kickbacks of any kind are unethical.

As I continued hiring people and increasing our production, it became clear that our trial run was working out well. I had staffed the factory with good people, our proximity to Cuba allowed us to be close to our tobacco suppliers, and the cigars coming out of our factory were better than ever.

In contrast, the labor situation in Cleveland had become intolerable. In January of 1954, after almost sixty years of manufacturing cigars in the Buckeye State, we decided to close our factory in Cleveland and transfer all our manufacturing operations to Tampa. I flew back north to tell our workers the unfortunate news.

Our Cleveland employees were used to hearing me give speeches on the factory floor. When I called a meeting that cold January morning, they probably expected me to announce that we had finally reached an agreement on a new contract. They were in for a shock.

"M & N is not competitive anymore," I began. "The union has made so many demands on us that it is difficult to sell our products and be competitive. Therefore, we have decided to close our operations in Cleveland and have another company make cigars for us. We are moving out of here on March first and we are going to start packing up. We're bringing in fifty trucks and we'd like your help loading them. I'm sorry it all worked out like this, but that's the way it is."

I walked out of the building to a huge outcry on the factory floor: shouts of protest, rumblings of disbelief. I wished things could have been different, but we had no other choice. I came back in the afternoon to repeat my speech to the night shift, but by then the news had already spread.

The union held an emergency meeting and decided to surround our factory with picket lines. It was a tense time. One day I was confronted by a union representative.

"We will never let you move out of here," he said. "We are going to stay here until you decide to keep this factory going. We will not let your trucks in. They won't even be able to get close to this building."

"It doesn't matter," I said. "Whether you let the trucks in or not, we are still going to close this factory."

As the first of March drew closer, a group of our employees formed a committee without the union and came to see me.

"We don't want you to leave," they told me. "We know the union hasn't been fair. If you keep the factory going we will vote the union out."

"I appreciate what you're trying to do," I said, "but it's too late—we are no longer viable as a business here. We've been the only cigar manufacturer in Cleveland for twenty-five years. We've done everything possible to make it work. We've made our decision and our decision is final."

I called a meeting of all our employees to explain our position.

"You have two choices," I said. "There is an unemployment insurance fund waiting for you in our state capital. That's $150,000 that belongs to you. If you choose to act responsibly and help us move out of here in an orderly fashion, that money is yours. If you choose to strike and refuse to help us move, you will not be eligible for unemployment insurance and you will receive nothing. It's your decision."

I didn't know what would happen. We had a caravan of fifty-three trailers coming to take all our equipment down to Florida. We couldn't possibly ship our entire factory's machinery and equipment without our employees' help.

When our trailers arrived at the factory, hundreds of employees defied the union and showed up to help. I had never felt such relief. Many of the employees approached me to say they understood why we were leaving and wished us well in our new home.

My brother Millard stayed in Cleveland as vice president of M & N, which then functioned as our sales organization. I became vice president of Standard Cigar Company in Tampa. My father, naturally, was president of both.

Al Korach and Frank Latnik were two key people who came down with us from Cleveland. My father had hired Al as an engineer in 1946. In time, Al became my right-hand man, overseeing engineering in the factory and helping me with the purchase of tobacco. Frank Latnik was a great asset too. He ran our sales order department for more than forty years. Both of these men were an integral part of our company. You are only as good as the people you employ.

My wife Elaine and I brought two children with us to Tampa. Our first-born surprised us when he came into the world on April 21, 1948, with blue eyes and blond hair. Elaine and I both had dark hair; neither of us has blue eyes.

When our pediatrician brought the baby to my wife's hospital room, he at first thought he had made a mistake. The doctor came into the room, looked at Elaine, looked at the baby, and then went back outside to double check the number on her door before asking skeptically, "Are you Newman?" Elaine said that yes, she was. "Where the heck did you get the blond?" he cracked.

In the days immediately following the birth of our son, Elaine and I tried to come up with a suitable name for him. While driving to work one day, the voice of one of Cleveland's most popular disc jockeys came over the radio, announcing, "This is Eric Marshall." I thought the name Eric—conjuring images of Eric the Viking, I suppose—had an appropriately Nordic sound to it, befitting our blue-eyed blond. We named him Eric Marshall Newman.

Eric the Baby Newman stars as the Baby New Year

My father didn't like the name Eric—he thought it sounded too Scandinavian—and insisted on calling my son Henry. I don't know why he liked the name Henry. He probably didn't care what the name was as long as it wasn't Eric. He went on calling him Henry for more than a year until he finally accepted the fact that we were not going to change Eric's name.

Eric was an adorable child, calm and good-natured, a complete delight. Almost three years after Eric was born, Elaine gave birth to our second son. This time, I wanted to be able to give our child a nickname. (Eric was always called Eric; there is no nickname for that.) Thus, we named Eric's younger brother, Robert, and always called him Bobby.

Bobby was born on February 11, 1951. He was a charger from the word go. Bringing him home from the hospital was an ordeal. When I tried to lay him down in the back seat of our car, he would not lie still. I had to walk him back and forth, pacing the whole hospital trying to get him to fall asleep. After an hour of this, people took notice, pointing to the wide-eyed baby and saying, "Look at that child!" They couldn't believe he was still awake after all that pacing. It was a sign of things to come. Bobby was never a good sleeper, a condition that only became worse after we moved to Tampa.

Eric and Bobby worked well together from the start

Tampa's heat and humidity are ideal conditions not only for tobacco, but for lightning as well. In fact, Tampa's claim to fame as the fine cigar capital of the world is rivaled only by its notoriety as the world's lightning capital.

Bobby was terrified of the thunder and lighting storms. When he was two years old, he would try to get into bed with us, but my wife wasn't too keen on the idea, so he crawled into bed with his brother. After awhile, whenever there was a lightning storm, Eric would automatically roll over and pull back the covers to make room for Bobby—without even waking up. My sons got along wonderfully. There wasn't anything they wouldn't do for each other.

Elaine was the disciplinarian at home. I was much more of a soft touch. I was determined not to make the same mistakes my father had made with me. When I was growing up, if I wasn't in school, I was indoors working. I wanted my sons to spend as much of their childhood outdoors as possible. I worked six days a week and didn't have as much time to spend with them as I would have liked, but I made sure my boys learned how to sail a boat, ride a horse, shoot an arrow, and catch a fish.

I wanted them to learn how to compete, to excel physically as well as mentally. Participating in sports is a great way to learn. Above all, I wanted my sons to develop enough confidence in themselves that they could talk softly and never feel the need to shout.

Eric and I early on in our
journey together

Taking time out with Eric

When Eric was twelve and Bobby was nine, we arranged for them to attend Camp Sequoyah, a summer camp in North Carolina. This was very important to me. I never had the opportunity to attend camp when I was a boy and I thought it would be a wonderful experience for them. They loved it so much that they went back every summer for many years. Eventually, both of them became camp counselors.

Eric became a Boy Scout too. Elaine would not allow the boys to start any activity unless they agreed to stick it out to the end. Eric devoted himself to the Boy Scouts whole-heartedly, advancing to the top rank of Eagle Scout. He was a natural born leader with an innate sense of fairness. Eric had a knack for looking at both sides of an argument and making good judgement calls.

I remember watching Eric and some of his friends playing baseball in our swimming pool one day when he was about ten years old. There was a big dispute about whether the ball was fair or foul and the boys on Eric's opposing team asked him to call it. They trusted him to be honest, even if it went against his own team.

Eric was always a humble person, never inclined to showoff. When I told him I was planning to give him a new car for his sixteenth birthday, he objected on the grounds that a used car would be more appropriate for a boy of his age! I insisted on a new car because I didn't want any problems with breakdowns. I bought him a brand new Ford Mustang and he really enjoyed driving it.

No description of Eric would be complete without mentioning his lifelong love of football. I took Eric to his first football game on our first Thanksgiving in Tampa. It had quite an impact on my six-year-old son. I doubt if he had a clue as to what was going on, but he sure got excited when our local high school team won six to nothing. We made an annual Thanksgiving Day tradition of going to the local football games for the next twenty years.

Eric played football in junior high school, high school, and college, and remains active in football to this day, refereeing local high school games. He makes an excellent football official precisely because he is so fair and objective.

Bobby was also a wonderful boy, but he was much more mischievous than his brother. Bobby knew how to have a good time. He also knew, ever since he could talk, how to get what he wanted from people. He'd just ask people to do things for him and they'd do it. It's a gift he still has. This makes him a very persuasive salesman.

But I'm getting ahead of myself. In the mid-1950s, my boys were still young children, and I was still trying to build a life for us in Tampa.

Our first summer in Tampa

En route with the boys to the
traditional Thanksgiving football game, 1956

Enjoying a moment with the next generation of cigar manufacturers

Elaine did not like Tampa in the beginning. Her first impression of the city was: "My God, I'm in a wasteland." There was no museum, the library was inadequate, and she couldn't stand the heat. This was made worse by the fact that our house didn't have air conditioning. Our builder had said we didn't need it with our house so close to the bay. Why I ever listened to him in the first place, I don't know. When my wife threatened to move back to Cleveland unless I did something about the heat, I had air conditioning installed right away.

Eventually, Elaine came to love Tampa. She is a real go-getter, and before I knew it, she was intimately involved in every kind of civic activity in the community. Six months after we had moved to Tampa, my wife called me and said, "By the way, we're having sixty people over for cocktails tonight." Elaine does everything fast. She drives fast, talks fast, eats fast, thinks fast. Soon, she was calling Tampa "my town."

One of the benefits of being a part of Tampa society was the opportunity to meet some wonderful people. When Benny Goodman came to town to play with the Tampa

Elaine and I proudly hosted Jack Benny when he performed in Tampa

Philharmonic, the orchestra board asked us to entertain him in our home. We were honored to have him; Elaine and I had grown up on Benny Goodman's music. We had a wonderful evening. I grilled some steaks and I remember Benny Goodman asking for a second helping of Elaine's famous cake roll.

We also had the great radio and television comedian, Jack Benny, to our house for dinner. Like Benny Goodman, he had come to Tampa to play with the Philharmonic. He was an accomplished violinist. He had a wonderful violin, a Stradivarius, and he would talk and crack jokes while he played. It was all part of his schtick. We were big fans of his, and he was a big fan of our cigars.

It was an exciting time for us. We were young, outgoing, always had places to go and people to see. Although I worked long hours and Elaine had her days full of charitable and civic commitments, we made a point of having dinner together as a family every weeknight. We also made a pact to spend every Saturday night together doing fun things. Sunday afternoons were reserved for visits to my parents for Sunday dinner. Elaine wasn't too happy about spending every Sunday with her in-laws, but she went along.

Statuesque and vivacious,
Elaine as a runway model in the 1950s

Bobby, like Elaine and myself, as enthusiastic
at play as at work

Back at the factory, my relationship with my father remained as contentious as ever. He continued to assert his authority in the most arbitrary ways, making decisions, as he had done with the fatal Cameo penny, without telling me ahead of time.

Our Arenco cigar machines from Sweden had been wonderful in their day, but they were now out-of-date. I bought six new machines from a man in Philadelphia and installed them in our factory, hoping to upgrade our old-fashioned equipment. I went out of town for several days and returned to the factory to find the machines were gone.

"What in the heck?" I said to my father. "I just bought these new machines and we haven't been running them! What happened?"

"I didn't like those machines," he said. "Carl Berger, a tobacco dealer from Cincinnati, was here the other day. I traded the cigar machines for some of his Puerto Rican filler tobacco."

I was livid.

"You shouldn't have done it," I said. There was nothing more I could think of to say.

This Puerto Rican filler tobacco caused some problems on the manufacturing end. The leaves had a tendency to curl up so that when we put them through our cigar machines, they created lumps in the cigars. We never had this problem with Cuban tobacco, which we prepared by placing it in big piles so that different leaves mixed together and formed good blends. We would have to prepare the Puerto Rican tobacco differently to eliminate the curls.

I thought a lot about this problem and came up with a solution. I had the tobacco straightened out on a conveyor belt and placed carefully in large cases, not piles. It took us a full week to get the job done. In time, I thought the leaves would flatten sufficiently to go through the machines successfully.

I returned to the factory a week later from a brief trip north and asked Raymond Lopez, the foreman in our filler department, to show me the tobacco. I wanted to see if it had curled back up again.

"Your father was here when you were out of town," Raymond said. "He made me take every one of those filler leaves you had straightened out and dump them on the floor. He said that's not the way to do it. He made me mix them all up and put them in big piles again."

This was the second time my father had undermined my efforts behind my back. He never let up, not even after I had gone home at the end of the day. He would call me on the telephone every single night with some new idea he wanted to discuss.

As we celebrated our first Christmas in Tampa in 1953, I made a speech to all of our employees at our annual Christmas party.

"Starting this January," I said, "everyone will receive an increase in pay."

Everyone indicated approval with cheers and applause.

"Furthermore, I am pleased to announce that you will receive an annual raise every January for as long as we remain in business. You can depend upon it."

There was more cheering and applause.

"If we run a successful company, we believe you should prosper along with us. When the time comes that we can't do that anymore, then all of us, including myself, will have to go and look for work elsewhere. We never want to make a profit on the backs of our employees."

Since that announcement in 1953, we have given our employees a pay raise every January. Unfortunately, in July of 1954 our cellophane machine operators decided they couldn't wait until January; they wanted their raises immediately and threatened to stop work until I gave in to their demands.

I reminded them that they would receive a raise at the end of the year, but they wouldn't listen. In hopes of persuading them to rethink their position, I went back to my office, grabbed a pile of job applications, and returned to the cellophane department, brandishing the applications before everyone.

"I'll tell you what," I said. "I have in my office a pile of applications just like these. If you don't want to go back to work, fine. You can just walk right out the front door and never come back."

Ten minutes later, the cellophane department supervisor called me in my office. "They all went back to work," she said.

It was frustrating dealing with these kinds of problems because I truly wanted our employees to feel the company was their home. If they needed advice or financial help, we gave it to them. And we were far more generous than Tampa's union cigar factories, not only in terms of salary, but also with medical benefits, holidays, vacations, and company parties.

As I always told our new employees, I was not against the unions. Rather, I simply wanted what was best for our employees and the company. I believe the owner of a company should have the right to run things the way he sees fit, as long as he treats his employees with respect and provides good working conditions. I believe I had the right idea, because almost no one has ever quit our company under my leadership. We pay our people well and, unlike other factories, treat them like family. No one seems to want to leave.

Nonetheless, I had to fight the union tooth and nail during our early years in Tampa. Standard Cigar Company was the only major non-union premium cigar factory in Tampa and the local union was under tremendous pressure from our competitors to get us into the union. Our competitors assumed we were undercutting them on wages. They didn't know we paid higher wages than they did. The union was accustomed to collectively bargaining for annual wage increases in all the Tampa cigar factories. Our competitors vowed to block all wage increases until Standard Cigar Company was unionized.

The union was desperate to organize our factory to ensure their annual wage increase, and for three years stationed people outside our factory trying to convince our workers to join.

Every afternoon during these union activities, there were five or six cars parked in front of our factory with union organizers behind the wheels waiting to follow our employees home.

When some of our employees were seen entering their homes, the union organizers would walk right up and knock on their doors, first making sure their husbands weren't home.

"May I please have a drink of water?" they asked.

Our employees were polite women, so they usually invited the men inside. The union organizer sat down, accepted a glass of water, and then shoved a union card in front of our employee's face.

"See your kids over there?" he said, gesturing to her children playing in the corner. "If you don't sign this union card, you may never see your children again."

This type of incident occurred with shocking regularity. When I first heard about these threats, I asked the Tampa police to come to our factory for a meeting with our employees. We encouraged everyone to call the police immediately if they were threatened.

The union was skilled in the art of harassment. Someone complained to the National Labor Relations Board (NLRB), a federal agency, that I was illegally threatening to fire any employee who joined the union. The allegation was totally untrue, but the NLRB went ahead and issued a court order prohibiting me from speaking to my own employees for a six-week period, standard practice when an employer was accused of this activity. I did my best to make light of this ridiculous situation: "See you in six weeks!" I said to our employees.

Things came to a head in the fall of 1958 when someone in our factory petitioned the NLRB for a union vote in our factory. The NLRB sent a representative down from Washington to discuss the matter with me.

"We have cards here signed by eighty percent of your employees indicating that they want to join the union," he said.

I couldn't believe so many of our employees wanted a union. It had to be forgery.

"Our employees didn't sign those cards," I said. I handed him paycheck stubs signed by all of our employees. "You need to verify those signatures."

The NLRB representative went back to his hotel to compare the signatures on the paystubs with those on his union cards. He came back to see me the next day.

"I compared all the signatures and have verified that they are legitimate," he said. "Since eighty percent of your employees want it, you have to let the union into your factory."

"You don't have that many signatures," I scoffed. "You might have a few, but you don't have eighty percent."

Although I repeatedly asked him to show me his cards, he steadfastly refused.

"I'll tell you something," I said. "You work for the NLRB. If you didn't come back here and tell me those signatures were legitimate, you'd be out of a job."

Seeing no alternative, I decided to settle things once and for all, no matter what the outcome.

"Let's have a union vote right away," I said.

It was nail-biting time. I didn't know what would happen. When the votes were tallied, it turned out that eighty-eight percent of our employees had voted against the union! I was overjoyed. The twelve percent that had voted for the union were run out of the building by the rest of our employees.

My victory with the union was bittersweet. That same year, my father died. He was 82 years old, less than a month away from his 83rd birthday.

J.C.'s lust for life burned until the end. The day he died on April 30, 1958, he rose at five o'clock in the morning, as usual. "The early bird catches the worm" was one of his favorite sayings. He used two alarm clocks to make sure he woke up early enough to perform his usual half-hour of exercise before heading to the office.

He arrived at work by 7 a.m. and began reviewing every piece of mail the company received that morning, writing instructions at the bottom of the most important letters as to how I should reply. After a full day at the office, he got into his brand-new car and drove off to the brand-new house he had just built. J.C. Newman was not a man preparing to die.

As he headed home, Tampa demonstrated once again that its moniker was well earned, and the lightning capital of the world unleashed a torrential thunderstorm. My father had a stroke in his car driving down the highway. It's a miracle he actually made it all the way home without causing an accident, although I did discover an almost unnoticeable bit of damage to the side of the garage.

He even managed to walk inside the house and lay down in the den. He told my mother he wasn't feeling well, so she called a doctor who lived next door and asked him to stop by on his way home. The doctor arrived less than an hour later and went into the den to check on J.C. He came out again almost immediately and sought my mother in the kitchen. "Your husband's dead," he said.

Bobby, age 3, with his grandfather, J.C.

Although she didn't realize it at the time, I think my mother suffered a mild heart attack on hearing the news. She died about one year later on September 1, 1959. She was buying a ticket for a movie with a friend when she suddenly fell ill. The manager of the theatre called an ambulance and she died on the way to the hospital. That's the way to go, in my opinion. I hope I can leave this world like my parents did, without spending any time in the hospital. My parents lived full lives until the very end.

I once asked my father what his father had left him when he died.

"My father had no material possessions or money to leave me," my father explained. "Instead, he left me something even more precious: the whole United States of America."

This was a meaningful gift for a man who had seen all his dreams come true in America. My father loved his adopted country with all his heart. As much as he believed in the value of a dollar, he never complained about paying taxes. He considered it a privilege to give back to the country that had given him so much. He had relished every opportunity—every obstacle—America offered up, seizing the American Dream with boundless energy and fierce determination. My father had been a force of nature. It was only fitting that nature should have marked his passing with her own display of sound and fury.

Millard and I face the future without J.C.

CIGAR OF THE KING OF SPAIN

*D*espite all our disagreements, my father had been my mentor. We had certainly argued more than I would have liked, but in the final analysis, we had made a good team: My strengths compensated for his weaknesses and vice versa. He taught me everything he knew about the cigar industry and more importantly, showed me that I could achieve anything I set my mind to if I believed in myself. He was sorely missed.

Just when I needed it most, a new mentor came into my life. I met Karl Cuesta in the late 1950s through the Cigar Manufacturers Association of Tampa, of which we were both members. Karl was in his early seventies, an elder statesman of the Tampa cigar industry. To my great good fortune, he took an instant liking to me.

Everyone loved Karl. His charm, wit, and engaging personality just naturally won people over. Karl was a southern gentleman. He was bilingual in English and Spanish and spoke both with a thick southern accent. Elaine and I often traveled with him to Cuba where we spent many memorable evenings enjoying the nightlife.

Karl took me under his wing and helped me become a full-fledged member of the Tampa community. In those days, Tampa had a lot of what I would call city fathers: a close-knit group of businessmen who exerted tremendous influence over the economic, political, and cultural life of the city. As part of this group, Karl was considered one of Tampa's most distinguished citizens. In fact, the Cuesta name was an icon in the city of Tampa.

Karl's father, Angel LaMadrid Cuesta, had been born in the mountains of northern Spain in 1858, where he spent his early life herding sheep. He left Spain for Cuba at the age of thirteen and, like my own father, achieved considerable success in the tobacco business while still in his teens. Angel Cuesta left Cuba for the United States in 1878, where he eventually settled in Atlanta, Georgia, and established his first cigar factory. With his partner, Peregino

Cuesta-Rey—the official cigar of the King of Spain

Rey, he established a cigar called Cuesta-Rey that soon became world-famous. Angel Cuesta moved his factory and family to Tampa in 1893, where his two sons, Karl and Angel, Jr., eventually became intimately involved in the family business.

Angel Cuesta Sr. continued to visit Spain, where his generosity as a philanthropist as well as his reputation for superb cigars brought him favor in the royal court. Cuesta and King Alfonso XIII of Spain became great friends, and it was said that Cuesta came and went from the royal palace "like Pedro in his own house." In time, King Alfonso knighted Cuesta and bestowed on him the title of official Cigar Purveyor to the Spanish King and Court.

When Angel LaMadrid Cuesta died in 1936, all the tobacco factories in Tampa closed in observance of his funeral. Karl and Angel, Jr., who both became good friends of mine, continued their father's legacy as respected leaders in the Tampa community. Their friendship meant a great deal to me.

Turn-of-the-century Cincinnati smokeshop selling Cuesta-Rey

Whenever he had the opportunity, Karl sponsored me into Tampa's inner circle and in 1961 proposed me for membership in the Rotary Club of Tampa, where I assumed his cigar manufacturer Rotary classification.

Then, in 1965, the Garcia Vega company, one of Tampa's leading cigar manufacturers, was purchased by Bayuk Cigar Company, one of the largest northern cigar corporations. The outgoing president of Garcia Vega had also been the president of the Tampa Cigar Manufacturers Association. When he left, Karl proposed me as the new president of the association and I was elected.

One of the other cigar manufacturers did not like the idea of my being president. He thought it should have been he. For the first few meetings after I was elected, I arrived about ten minutes early. The funniest thing was that this person always arrived ahead of me and sat in my seat at the head of the table, as if he were the one running the meeting. I soon learned to arrive fifteen minutes early instead of ten, so that I got my seat. He wasn't too happy about it.

To the best of my knowledge, the other members were happy with my performance as president. One of my great successes was spearheading a campaign to promote Tampa as the Fine Cigar Capital of the World. The campaign was extensive: We placed large billboards at major approaches into the city proclaiming Tampa "The Fine Cigar Capital of the World"; we put up cigar exhibits at Tampa International Airport; we placed a cigarmaker at Tampa's Busch Gardens theme park; and we sponsored cigar appreciation luncheons. All of these tactics helped enhance the image of the Tampa cigar industry.

Perhaps my most important contribution as president of the association was to give our Tampa cigar industry a stronger voice in the state legislature. We never used lobbyists, but I did arrange for the association to host an annual luncheon for the legislative delegation from our county. Mostly, it was a forum for our legislators to hear our industry's concerns and for them to share their thoughts about the important issues of the day. We had some lively discussions.

At the end of each luncheon, I made a point of reminding them that we had no lobbyists. "All we ask is that if someone should introduce a bill adversely affecting our Tampa cigar industry, you just let them know that cigars are your home industry and do everything you can to fight for us."

I retired as president of the Tampa Cigar Manufacturers Association in January of 1998 after more than thirty years of service. My son, Eric, is now president of the association. The

One of the billboards from our Tampa Cigar Manufacturers Association campaign

Tampa cigar industry no longer advertises collectively, but to this day, Florida remains one of the few states in the Union that does not tax cigars. I will always remain grateful to Karl Cuesta for recommending me to a position that allowed me to do some good for the entire Tampa cigar industry.

I established another important friendship in Tampa just a few years after I first met Karl. Bob Franzblau had only lived in Tampa for about two years when I met him at a dinner party in 1960. One Monday morning he came to see me at the factory, asking if he could buy five boxes of cigars. The next Monday he wanted ten boxes. The following Monday it was fifteen.

Finally, I asked: "What are you doing with all these cigars?"

"I have some friends back in New York who keep asking me to send them Tampa-made cigars."

Bob had recently sold his building supply business and was looking for a new line of work. I had an idea about what he might try.

"Why don't you go into the cigar mail order business?"

He immediately agreed that it was a good idea. Together we looked through the local telephone book and found a company that suited Bob's needs. Thompson Cigar Company, founded in the early 1900s, owned a mail order distribution service in Tampa and a cigar factory about forty miles away in Bartow, Florida. In 1961, I helped Bob acquire it. Part of the deal was that M & N purchase Thompson's entire tobacco inventory and some of its manufacturing equipment. I then became the exclusive manufacturer for Thompson cigars.

Under Bob's new leadership, Thompson's mail order business took off. Within a few short years, it became one of the largest mail order cigar companies in the country, and our number one customer. With almost twenty percent of our cigar production earmarked for

The Cuesta and Newman families, from left: Noretta Cuesta, Elaine, Karl Cuesta, me, and Angel Cuesta, Jr.

Thompson, I eventually became concerned that we were too dependent upon each other for our own good. I convinced Bob that it was in both of our best interests to find Thompson an additional supplier and I introduced Bob to some of our competitors in Tampa. Thompson continued to flourish and by the early 1990s, became one of the largest customers for almost every cigar manufacturer and importer in the U.S. To this day, Bob and I are still the best of friends.

After my father's death, I redoubled my efforts to acquire a brand that would make us a player in the high-priced, premium cigar market. I had been searching for a nationally recognized premium cigar brand for quite some time. My acquisition would have to fulfill two criteria. First, the brand had to have a reputation for quality that had never been compromised, a tall order considering how many brands had lost favor with cigar smokers as manufacturers cheapened quality to compete at lower prices. Second, the brand had to have a national distribution, particularly in the South, where our presence was still minimal.

As luck, or fate, would have it, the brand that Karl Cuesta's father had established in 1884 fit the bill completely. Cuesta-Rey was a name recognized all over the world. The label had never been hurt like many other brands that had been reduced in retail price.

I knew that Karl was concerned about Cuesta-Rey's future. He wanted to make sure the brand continued after he passed away. It occurred to me that with one stroke, I could make Karl's wish—and my father's—come true. I made Karl a proposition.

"Cuesta-Rey is one of the best cigar brands going," I said. "I'd like to help keep it that way. It was always my father's dream to own a premium cigar brand and I'm looking to acquire one. Cuesta-Rey is perfect, and I'd like to buy your business. You get the satisfaction of knowing that Cuesta-Rey is in the best possible hands, and I get to see my father's dream come true. I assure you we will always maintain the highest quality, and I think I can actually make Cuesta-Rey even more successful."

After I made him a substantial offer, Karl smiled and said, "I like your proposition, Stanford."

Before we could consummate the deal, I had to make sure that Cuesta-Rey's largest distributor, the Eli Witt Company, would continue to distribute the cigar after the brand had changed ownership. Eli Witt's continuing distribution of Cuesta-Rey in the ten Southeastern states they serviced was essential.

So, Karl and I went to see Hoyt Woodberry, president of Eli Witt. Mr. Woodberry agreed to keep Cuesta-Rey in his stable of brands—it had been the first cigar Eli Witt had ever sold when the company started its retail business in 1918—if I met three conditions.

"First, I want to make sure that you won't let the quality decline after you take ownership," Woodberry said. I assured him that I would never sacrifice the quality of the cigars.

"Second, as you probably know, I'm not just a tobacco distributor. I also manufacture the Hav-a-Tampa cigar brand," he said.

Hav-a-Tampa was a very popular cigar; I knew it well.

"I have no salesmen of my own. Instead, I expect your salesmen to sell Hav-a-Tampa before they sell Cuesta-Rey. I ask all of the manufacturers I work with to sell Hav-a-Tampa before they sell their own brands. When one of your salesmen visits a store, if there is a possibility of selling only one box of cigars, they have to sell Hav-a-Tampa before any other cigars."

That sounded reasonable to me.

"Finally, you can put as many salesmen on Cuesta-Rey as you like, but you can't ask any of my accounts to take out one of your competitor's brands and replace it with Cuesta-Rey. It wouldn't be fair to the other manufacturers I carry. If I find out that any of your salesmen are doing this, they will not be welcome ever again in any of our fifty-five distribution houses from here to Texas."

If I had been in Mr. Woodberry's position, I would have expected the same thing. He had to protect his relationships with the other manufacturers he represented. I agreed to abide by his conditions and in September of 1958 the deal was consummated.

I bought Karl's tobacco, whatever equipment we needed, and any label that had a Cuesta-Rey name on it. Karl had some other brands—White Heather, La Unica, and a few others—that I acquired in the process. Karl wanted to give me some of his other brands that were registered in Cuba, like El Rey del Mundo and Sancho Panza. "Just pay me for the labels," he said.

The brand that made us players in the premium cigar market

"I'll buy them," I said, "but I'll throw them away. I'm interested in only one brand—Cuesta-Rey."

Karl sold these other brands to someone else. Over the years, they became quite valuable. Looking back, I admit it was a mistake not to buy them.

Cuesta-Rey was probably the single most important acquisition in our company history. With Cuesta-Rey, I was finally able to make my father's dearest dream come true and establish our company as a premium cigar manufacturer.

Rigoletto, which had been our premium-priced brand, was repositioned as a medium-priced cigar. Cuesta-Rey became our premium brand, and gave us our best opportunity at finally becoming a full-fledged national cigar company.

In truth, while Cuesta-Rey had had a good reputation, it was not a major player in the premium cigar industry at the time we acquired it. While there was some business in the twenty-six-cent category, many Cuesta-Rey cigars sold for only ten cents. The total volume of business was about four or five million cigars.

My goal was to establish Cuesta-Rey firmly as a leading premium cigar. My first tactic was to introduce the Cuesta-Rey Palma Supreme at twenty-six cents to compete with the four leading twenty-six-cent brands: Bering, Gold Label, Garcia Vega, and Perfecto Garcia. This didn't work because it was a "me-too" strategy. People would not buy Cuesta-Rey at twenty-six cents when there was nothing to differentiate it from the competition.

The disappointing response to Cuesta-Rey Palma Supreme only strengthened my long-held belief that I was at war: My competitors were my enemies, and they were much bigger than we were. If your enemy has a hundred thousand soldiers, and you only have five thousand, what do you do? Do you come out with the same products at the same price? Your enemies will roll over you if you try. You cannot attack them directly. You have to go around them, do something different, be original. I had gone against my philosophy when I introduced Cuesta-Rey at twenty-six cents. I would not repeat my mistake.

I did not believe our problem had anything to do with quality. I thought consumers would like our cigars if we could just get people to try them. Of course, persuading people to convert to a different brand is extremely difficult.

A fellow will try a new cigar, like it, and never buy it again. He goes back to the brand he is used to. It's like a marriage. A man can go out with a girl on the side and think she's the best woman in the world, spend the whole night with her, but in the morning he's forgotten her name and he goes right back to Mamma. I often told our salesmen that we were only going to get as many conversions to our brand as there were divorces.

In order to get people to divorce their mammas in favor of Cuesta-Rey, I came up with an entirely new premium cigar concept. We took two bundles of twenty-five Palma-shaped cigars and packed them "in the round." (At the time, almost all Tampa-made cigars were pressed into square shapes.) We then packaged our cigars without cellophane inside a handsome cedar box, as was the custom in Cuba.

I named this new Cuesta-Rey cigar, "Number 95" (the year my father founded J.C. Newman Cigar Company.) It was one of the first numbered cigars ever marketed in the United States. I thought the number lent a touch of class to the brand and helped distinguish it from the competition.

More importantly, putting a number on our cigar bands would help consumers identify this cigar more easily. I had always believed there were too many cigar sizes on the market, and because most cigar bands featured only a brand name and not a number to identify the size of the cigar, consumers were easily confused. They still are today.

This is what happens. A person goes into a cigar store and asks for one of his favorite brands. The tobacconist brings him a cigar that is much larger than his customer prefers. The customer tries to describe the size he's looking for, but can't remember the exact frontmark. Consumer and retailer are reduced to trial and error.

Putting a number on Cuesta-Rey was my attempt to make it easier for consumers to identify sizes. My hope was that cigar smokers would catch on to the number and begin asking for a 95 instead of a Cuesta-Rey. Eventually, they did. Every time I asked someone what cigar he was smoking and was told, "95," I considered it a personal victory. We were practically the only cigar manufacturer to put size identification numbers on our cigar bands.

We introduced Cuesta-Rey No. 95 at thirty-five cents, pretty much the highest price point on the market in 1959. I was immensely gratified by the success of our cigars. I believe the concept worked because, while 95 was different from anything else on the market, the Cuesta-Rey name was familiar enough to cigar smokers that they didn't feel they were taking a chance on a totally unknown brand.

Naturally, the fact that Cuesta-Rey cigars were made entirely of Cuban tobacco was a major factor in the brand's success. By now, Cuban tobacco was so important to our reputation that we used 100-percent Cuban tobacco in all of our cigars, as did the entire cigar industry in Tampa.

The country that produced this prized tobacco was an exotic, charming, sometimes dangerous place. Just a short distance from Tampa, Cuba was the setting for some of my most memorable experiences in the cigar industry.

Cuesta-Rey No. 95

CUBA

I spent a great deal of time in Cuba during the 1950s, traveling to Havana at least once a month for meetings with tobacco dealers and packers. My travels often took me to the province of Pinar del Rio where, to this day, some of the finest Cuban tobacco is grown.

My visits to Cuban tobacco plantations always began the same way: The tobacco grower led me straight to the largest pile of cow manure on his farm. "Just look at that nice big pile!" he would say, beaming with pride. As my tour of the plantation continued, the farmer inevitably called my attention to every immense pile we came across.

This never ceased to amaze me. Why, I wondered, did Cuban tobacco growers take such pride in the size of their manure piles? One day, I asked one of my tobacco friends: "Why do the farmers always show me their piles of cow manure?"

"They believe that the quality of the tobacco is directly related to the quantity of fertilizer used," he explained.

The soil surely needed as much fertilization as it could get. Most of the land in Cuba was worn out from over-cultivation and depleted of nutrients.

Another thing that puzzled me was that the uppermost leaves of Shade tobacco plants were never harvested. These thick top-leaves, called the corona, were considered unusable and routinely plowed under. This struck me as a waste of potentially good tobacco. I had a hunch that the corona leaves might be turned into quality wrapper tobacco if properly nurtured.

I convinced one of the Cuban plantation owners I knew to continue irrigating his tobacco after most of the leaves were harvested to see if the corona leaves would continue to grow satisfactorily. Despite his strenuous objection that this would never work, the corona leaves indeed grew longer and produced a light, flavorful wrapper tobacco. Since corona leaves were usually not picked, growers were willing to sell them to us at a very reasonable price.

CORONA {

The tobacco plant

We used this tobacco to manufacture moderately priced light green cigars, a very different type of cigar than the traditional Cuban smoke.

Most cigars made from Cuban tobacco, including Cuesta-Rey, used a dark, chocolate-brown wrapper, which gave them a robust, rich taste. After World War II, cigars made with a light green wrapper, perceived to be milder in taste, became popular among cigar smokers. These cigars were hard to come by. Only about five percent of Cuba's total wrapper tobacco production is naturally light green in color when cured according to the traditional process, which involves hanging the tobacco leaves in barns with the window slats open, allowing fresh air to dry the leaves for a period of about six to eight weeks. Therefore, to meet the increasing demand for light green wrapper cigars, a few Cuban tobacco farmers came up with an elaborate process in 1945 called fire curing, in which fresh green wrapper leaves were heated with charcoal in sealed barns and fast-cured over a seventy-two-hour period to seal their green color. Light green tobacco wrapper cured by this process became known as candela.

We manufactured two cigar brands using corona candela wrapper tobacco: Havana Coronitas and Rigoletto Palma Grandes. I came up with a successful marketing gimmick to promote Rigoletto Palma Grandes, packaging one free cigar attached to packs of five. This "buy one pack—get one cigar free" concept worked wonders. In time, we were selling a quarter of a million of these cigars a day. We had to purchase twenty more cigar machines and add a night shift to fill the orders.

One of my experiences with Carlos Toraño, the packer who supplied most of our corona tobacco, is indicative of the relationships I developed in Cuba. I was visiting Carlos at his tobacco farm in Cuba to purchase a substantial amount of candela tobacco for next year's cigars. The tobacco would have to be specially grown for me and had to be delivered promptly within one year's time. I had drawn up a contract and brought it with me along with a check for $250,000 as a down payment on the $1,000,000 I expected to pay for the entire lot of this tobacco.

"I have a contract and a deposit I want to give you," I explained to Carlos. "I want to make sure I receive your tobacco a year from now or I will have serious problems."

"Let me explain something," he replied. "We don't have contracts in Cuba. We do the deal with a handshake or not at all. There are very few non-Cubans that I like, but I do like you. If I didn't, I wouldn't do business with you."

Carlos didn't want a contract, nor did he want my money. Not until he delivered the tobacco a year later.

Most of the Cubans I knew were like him: the kind of people who, if they liked you, would give you the shirt off their backs—and if they didn't like you, would just as soon shoot you.

Fortunately, almost all of the Cuban tobacco growers I worked with took a liking to me and we developed great friendships.

J.C. and Gladys cool off at The
Hotel Nacional in Havana, Cuba

Vintage postcard for Cuban tourism

I received my Cuban tobacco right on schedule and stuck to my end of the bargain by paying for it on time as well. In my experience it is just as important to stick to an oral agreement as it is to a written one, if not more so.

I learned another important lesson in Cuba in 1946 while eating at a prominent restaurant in Havana called La Floridita with my father and one of our Cuban tobacco suppliers. We were finishing our coffee when a man walked in off the street, approached the table next to us, picked up a chair, and smashed it over the unsuspecting diner's head. After things quieted down, I asked our dinner companion if he could explain what had just happened.

"Those two gentlemen are politicians," he said. "They were in a debate on television last night and one of them took great offense at what the other said about him. I'll tell you

Harvesting tobacco in Cuban fields

It wasn't all work in Cuba

something. If that man practiced what I practice, he never would have been hit over the head like that."

"What do you mean?" I asked.

"I never turn my back to the door," he explained. "You never know who's going to come at you."

Ever since that incident at La Floridita it has always been my habit to take a seat facing the door whenever I go to a restaurant.

The best times I ever had in Cuba were the times I spent with my wife enjoying the nightlife in Havana. It was spectacular. The sheer number of restaurants, cafes, nightclubs, and casinos amazed me. Neon lights flashed everywhere at night. We strolled along Havana's broad, tree-lined avenues, pausing to enjoy the many plazas decked with flowers.

My Cuban friends took us to the most unbelievable nightclubs: hot spots like the Tropicana, Monmartre, and San Souci. The Tropicana was situated outdoors. After dinner, lights would come up in the trees, revealing dancing girls perched in the branches. They really knew how to put on a show.

They also knew a thing or two about service. In the nightclubs, it was considered discourteous to mix someone else's drink. The waiters gave you a whole bottle of whatever you ordered, like in the Wild West, and let you pour your own drinks. At the end of the evening, they measured how much you had consumed and charged accordingly. It struck me as a fine way to treat your customers, although I never drank very much myself.

Cuba was not all fun and games, of course. Since the early 1950s, the name of Fidel Castro had been on everyone's mind. The government at that time, a dictatorship under the rule of Fulgenco Batista, was considered corrupt and suppressive. Castro had become a popular revolutionary figure by the mid-1950s, waging guerrilla warfare on the Batista government from his hideout in the Sierra Mountains.

I learned a little something about this in 1957 during a visit with Carlos Toraño, who had become one of my most important Havana tobacco suppliers. Carlos had kept me waiting for hours in his office. When he finally showed up, I said, "My gosh, Carlos, I've been waiting here for a long time. What on earth have you been up to?"

"I'm sorry to have kept you waiting. I was at the bank this afternoon counting pesos to send up to the mountains to Castro." He told me he was sending Castro 100,000 pesos, equivalent to $100,000 at the time.

"Why are you doing this?" I asked. "You have a nice life down here, a beautiful home, beautiful nightclubs, a successful business, lots of tourists. Why do you want to change the government?"

"The Batista government is corrupt," Carlos said. "A big chunk of our taxes goes directly into the tax collectors' pockets, instead of to the government. Castro promises when he takes over, we will have an honest government with fair taxation."

It sounded a little too good to be true, but I kept my mouth shut. Castro's attacks on the Batista regime intensified until, in January of 1959, Castro's army invaded Havana and Batista fled the country. Castro proclaimed that a dictator would never again rule Cuba.

His promise was short-lived. Not long after the revolution, Castro began taking control of Cuba's major industries, including the tobacco industry. Castro himself showed up at Carlos Toraño's office in Havana to share the good news. Accompanied by a soldier brandishing a machine gun, Castro barged into Carlos's office and confronted him.

"We are taking over your business," Castro said.

"Listen, Fidel. I've been a good friend to you. Remember how I always sent money to you up in the mountains? Please don't do this to me."

"You're just a damn fool," Castro said. "Now get out!"

"I'm not going to get out!"

Castro turned to the soldier and said, "Tell Carlos what happened to the last businessman who refused to cooperate."

"I shot him," the soldier said matter-of-factly, as he adjusted his machine gun.

Carlos backed off and Castro took over his business. Carlos eventually settled in Madrid, Spain, a popular destination for Cuban exiles. Many more fled to Nicaragua, Honduras, and the Dominican Republic. I met Carlos in Madrid in 1965, when he told me of his frightening encounter with Fidel Castro.

All of us in Tampa's Clear Havana cigar industry continued to buy Cuban tobacco after the revolution. The only difference was that now we were dealing with the Castro government. We didn't have much choice. Cuban tobacco was our lifeblood. Besides,

Fidel Castro

none of us in Tampa had any idea that a United States embargo of Cuban tobacco was just around the corner.

The Tampa cigar manufacturers stored most of their tobacco in warehouses in Havana and had it sent to them as needed on a ship called *The Privateer* that traveled between Havana and Tampa twice a week.

One man convinced me to prepare for the day when *The Privateer* might no longer be allowed to bring Cuban tobacco into the United States: Angel Oliva, one of the most prominent leaf tobacco dealers in Havana and Tampa, and one of the fairest, most honorable businessmen I knew. He was convinced that the Cuban situation was only going to get worse. He believed the U.S. would soon be forced to embargo Cuban tobacco in retaliation for Castro's increasingly hostile conduct. In July of 1960, Angel invited me to visit a tobacco grower and packer in Quincy, Florida, the same tobacco-growing region

I had turned to when Connecticut Shade became prohibitively expensive after World War II.

At first, I declined Angel's invitation. Why buy Florida tobacco when I could still get it from Cuba? But Angel was persistent. He practically dragged me to Quincy, even paid for my plane ticket. In Quincy, we discussed the possibility of growing candela wrapper. The tobacco dealers did not want to produce the candela tobacco unless someone was prepared to buy it. I agreed to put up the money for an experiment to produce about 100 bales.

When the tobacco was ready, I took fifty bales and encouraged Angel to take the other fifty as samples to show other cigar manufacturers. I wanted to make this wrapper tobacco popular so that it would be accepted by consumers and the industry. Most of the manufacturers wouldn't even look at it. They quickly changed their tune when, four months later, the embargo Angel predicted came to fruition. The other Tampa cigar manufacturers then followed my lead, placing orders with Angel Oliva for more than 6,000 bales of Quincy candela wrapper.

None of us knew exactly what was in store in the months leading up to the embargo, and I continued to visit Cuba on a regular basis to check up on my tobacco. During my first trip to Havana after the revolution, Castro's presence was inescapable. Every television in every restaurant was broadcasting Castro's speeches for hours on end, day after day. Castro would show a picture of a downtown building and say, "This is what I got for you from the crooks who were running our government. This is your building now!" Everyone in the restaurants—from the businessmen having lunch to the waiters and busboys serving them—all stopped what they were doing and cheered. Meanwhile, Castro's enemies were being rounded up and thrown in jail, or worse.

EMBARGO

By 1960, it was clear that Castro was going Communist. He had made overtures to the Soviet Union, and was becoming quite cozy with Khrushchev. In June of that year, the Kennedy Administration declared an embargo on Cuban sugar. The writing was on the wall, and a tobacco embargo couldn't be far off. In December of 1960, just weeks before Kennedy severed diplomatic relations with Cuba, I made my last trip to Havana, accompanied by Al Korach, the engineer my father had hired, who by now had become my right-hand man.

I knew I was in trouble from the moment we showed our passports to the customs officer at the Havana airport.

"He can go on, but you must wait here," the officer said to me. I told Al to go ahead and wait for me outside. I was escorted to a jail cell at the airport by a guard who spoke about as much English as I did Spanish, which is to say, not much.

"Wait here," he said. I didn't have to wait long. Soon enough, a soldier came in, looked me up and down, and said: "Take off all your clothes."

I reluctantly complied while he reviewed my papers. I was then subjected to a humiliating strip-search. Of course, he found nothing. I was allowed to put my clothes back on and left alone in the cell, where I spent the next eight hours wondering what in God's name was going to happen to me. I don't know if I was more relieved or frightened when another soldier finally arrived. He was barely eighteen years old. I immediately spoke up.

"I don't know what you're holding me for. I'm here to buy tobacco. Here's my briefcase," I said, pulling it out for him.

Cuban cigar manufacturing

"I'll tell you why you're here," he said. Thank God he spoke English. "We've been monitoring your visits to Cuba and we're concerned that you've been coming here so regularly. We believe you may be involved in anti-Castro activities." He knew exactly how many times I had been to Cuba since Castro took over.

"I have nothing to do with politics," I said. "I'm here to buy tobacco. There's a fellow in the tobacco business who has been waiting for the last eight hours to pick me up. His name is Norberto Junco."

I produced stationery, letters, everything I had that substantiated my claim. As he looked them over, recognition dawned on his face.

"You know, I used to live right next door to the Junco's plantation," he said. "My parents still live there. What you're telling me is true. Stay here and I'll go get my superior."

Cathedral, Havana

He came back with his superior officer, who was very apologetic. He explained again why I had been detained, saying that they had to be cautious with anyone making so many trips back and forth between the U.S. and Cuba.

"My subordinate says his parents have a farm right next to where you're going, and he's willing to vouch for you. You're free to go."

When I finally arrived at the Hotel Nacional, it was almost midnight. I called Elaine to tell her what had happened. She wanted me to come home on the next flight, but I said as long as I was here, I might as well do what I came for. I told her I would be back at the end of the week after visiting several tobacco plantations. When Elaine started telling me what was going on back in Tampa, a curious thing happened.

"We had a few guests at our house from Mexico today," she was saying. As soon as she said the word Mexico, z-z-z-t—I heard a strange buzzing on the line. Our phone was being tapped. Someone was listening to our conversation. It was unnerving.

"Elaine, I've got to hang up," I said, inventing some excuse about there being someone at the door.

I got into bed and tried to sleep. About a half-hour later, I heard a sound outside my door. Click. Click. There was no one else staying on my floor; the place was empty. Who was outside my door? Then I heard it again. Click. Click. Click.

I jumped out of bed, crept as silently as I could to my door, and put my ear up against it. The sound didn't repeat. I went back to bed and spent a fitful night tossing and turning, but the sound never came again. I'll never know if it was just my imagination or whether there really was someone outside my door.

The rest of the week passed without incident and I arrived at the Havana airport on a Saturday morning for my eight o'clock flight back to Miami feeling a mixture of relief and anxiety. I was glad to be going home, but I wasn't there yet. I worried that it might be even harder to get out of Cuba than it had been to get in.

As soon as I arrived at the airport, it was announced that my plane was delayed for half an hour. Nothing unusual in that, I thought. But then another half-hour delay was announced, and another and another, until I found myself still waiting at the airport at four o'clock in the afternoon.

Finally, it was announced that the plane was ready for boarding. I was so glad to get out of there. The atmosphere in the airport was tense, to say the least. Thousands of Cubans were trying to get out of the country and Castro was cracking down, trying to halt the embarrassing flood of Cubans to America. Every person of Cuban nationality waiting to board my flight was taken out of line and strip-searched to make sure they weren't taking any pesos out of the country.

I didn't begin to relax until I was onboard the plane. When we began taxiing toward the runway, I thought my troubles were over. I was wrong. Just when the plane was about to take off, it stopped at the edge of the runway, turned around, and headed back to the terminal. The plane stopped and two policemen came on board.

The two of them slowly walked down the aisle. I was sitting at the back of the plane, trying to reassure myself that they couldn't possibly be looking for me. As they came closer and closer to where I was sitting, I became convinced that they were after me; something I had said at customs perhaps or a remark overheard at one of the tobacco farms I had visited made someone suspicious. Maybe they didn't like the idea of my wife entertaining visitors from Mexico?

The two policemen stopped right in front of me. I was sweating bullets. I prepared myself for the ordeal ahead, rehearsing what I would say to clear myself, hoping I wouldn't be subjected to another strip-search. I just about had a heart attack when the officer on my side of the aisle extended his arms, as if to pull me out of my seat. Instead, he grabbed the fellow

Smokeshop in Havana

Santiago, Cuban Carnival Day singer

sitting right in front of me and dragged him off the plane. My immense relief was tempered only by my concern for the poor fellow they had taken.

This whole ordeal was also having an effect on my twelve-year-old son, Eric. He was waiting for me at the Tampa airport and had grown increasingly worried as the delays piled up. Earlier in the week, he had made a playful comment to me over the phone about Castro, something to the effect of "How's Fidel doing?" As he waited for me at the Tampa airport for hour after hour, he began to imagine that whatever had happened to me was all his fault. The poor kid thought his innocent comment had somehow caused the Cuban authorities to arrest me. Eric was so distraught, he called his mother, who came to the airport and took him home. Needless to say, we were all relieved when I finally made it back safely. I promised myself I was never going back to Cuba.

I couldn't have gone back even if I had wanted to. On January 3, 1961, after sending out his press secretary, Pierre Salinger, to buy every Montecristo cigar he could find in the city of Washington, President Kennedy severed diplomatic relations with Cuba and announced a full trade embargo. I actually met J.F.K. once, in Cuba of all places. This was in 1957 when he was still a Senator. I was waiting in line to register at my hotel in Havana when Senator Kennedy got in line directly behind me. He looked like a giant—very tall—and had a commanding presence. We had a short but pleasant conversation, mostly about how much we both enjoyed Cuba, and he struck me as a very nice man.

In the final days leading up to the embargo, I knew the end was coming and did my best to prepare for the inevitable, arranging for an especially large shipment of Cuban tobacco worth half a million dollars. When *The Privateer* left for Havana with my $500,000 letter of credit from the Royal Bank of Canada, one of the few banks still doing business in Cuba, I fully expected this to be her final voyage.

The next day, I received a devastating telegram from the Secretary of State, advising me that a Cuban trade embargo was immediately in effect. Any attempt to transport tobacco from Cuba to a U.S. port would result in the immediate confiscation of both the tobacco and the ship.

It was too late for *The Privateer* to simply turn around and come home. She had already docked in Havana. I called Higinio Miguel, my tobacco agent in Cuba, and asked him to do everything in his power to prevent the tobacco from being loaded onto the ship. He promised to do his best.

Our mutual fear was that even if the tobacco were not loaded onto the ship, Cuban government officials might force *The Privateer*'s captain to sign shipping documents indicating he had received the tobacco. This would allow the Cuban government to collect the $500,000 and keep the tobacco. The situation in Cuba was so volatile that they might even compel the captain to sign at gunpoint.

I had made quite a few friends in Cuba over the years. As fate would have it, some of them happened to be loading tobacco for the Cuban government when *The Privateer* arrived at Havana harbor. When they learned that Stanford Newman had requested that his tobacco not be loaded onto the ship, they happily complied, and the captain was not forced to sign the shipping documents. *The Privateer* returned safely to Tampa with my half a million dollars secure. The captain told me later that we surely would have lost the ship, the tobacco, and the money if not for my friends' help.

We had managed to avert disaster for the time being, but the long-term effects of the embargo would have to be faced. At first, we thought the embargo would last only about six months or so, but as I write these words nearly forty years later, the embargo is still in effect. As the embargo sank in as a permanent fact of life, it had a chilling effect on the entire Clear Havana cigar industry in Tampa. The consensus was that this was the end of Tampa's premium cigar business. Many of my colleagues in Tampa simply gave up and put their businesses up for sale.

I tried to reassure myself with the knowledge that my father had seen us through even worse situations than this. What would he have done if he were still here? One thing was certain: He would not have given up. He would have found some way to keep the company going. As he so often reminded me, there was always a way out of a bad situation. I resolved that, no matter what it took, the company my father started in 1895 was not going to fail on my watch.

It was hard to remain confident when so many of the other family-owned cigar manufacturers in Tampa were bailing out. One by one, they sold out to the big northern cigar corporations. Morgan Cigar Company was sold to Gradiaz Annis, makers of Gold Label. Gradiaz Annis was then sold to General Cigar Company. Garcia Vega was sold to Bayuk Cigar Company, and Perfecto Garcia to United States Tobacco Company. This all occurred between about 1961 and 1964. Eventually, in 1986, Corral Wodiska, makers of Bering, was sold to Swisher.

I received my share of offers, but I was not interested in selling. The offers meant nothing to me because I still had confidence in our business.

At the same time, I was approached by Cuban cigar manufacturers whose businesses had been overtaken by the Castro government. They had no money and wanted to sell me their Cuban brand names. These were not just any old cigar brands, either. They were offering me famous brands.

"Just pay us a royalty of one dollar per thousand cigars," they said.

It was a tempting offer, but I knew better.

"Let me ask you one question," I said. "Who owns the registration for these brands in the United States?"

"The Cuban government," was the answer.

"I am not going to make cigar brands that are owned by the Cuban government in the United States," I said. "Let's say we start making cigars in Tampa under these brand names. If a year from now the embargo is lifted and we start doing business with Castro again, he's not going to like it that we're using his brands. Furthermore, if I manufacture one of these Cuban brands, I can only sell it in the U.S., since the Cuban government still owns the brand registration for the rest of the world. I have a good brand in Cuesta-Rey, which we can sell all over the world without restrictions."

Cuesta-Rey had once been made in Cuba, yet the Cuban government had never registered the trademark. Cuesta-Rey was one of the few brands being made in Tampa with a Cuban brand heritage that could be sold all over the world.

Some of our competitors were happy to snap up these Cuban brands. As I predicted, to this day, the U.S. cigar companies making such brands as Hoyo de Monterrey, H. Upmann, and Partagas can't sell them outside the United States because Cuba owns the worldwide trademarks. I'm glad I had the foresight to refuse those offers.

Immediately after the embargo, Garcia Vega began advertising the slogan, "Yes, We Still Have Havana," on all their cigar boxes. They never actually said they still used Havana in their cigars. For all I knew, they might have had just a single bale of Havana tobacco in storage. I told our tobacco department supervisor to set aside one bale of Cuban tobacco so that if anyone ever asked me whether we still had Havana, I could reply in the affirmative. To this day that one bale of Cuban filler tobacco is still sitting in the basement of our factory.

Meanwhile, I was still stuck with the problem of how to keep our business going without Cuban tobacco. Our reputation rested almost entirely on the fact that our cigars were made from 100 percent Cuban tobacco. What's a manufacturer to do when his sole supply of raw material is suddenly cut off? I had a substantial stockpile of Cuban tobacco, but it would run out in less than two years. I had to find a new source of high quality tobacco and the clock was ticking.

THE FRENCH CONNECTION

The answer to my prayers came in the mail one day in 1961 when a nondescript package arrived at my office from Stephen Kahn, the president of Hofer Tobacco, a New York subsidiary of the prestigious Dutch tobacco dealer A.L. van Beck. Inside the package were samples of a dark, chocolate-brown wrapper tobacco, and it was not from Cuba. This tobacco had been grown in the former French colonies of Cameroon and the Central African Republic.

The smell, the look, the feel of this Cameroon tobacco was exceptional. I felt my hopes rising—could this be the replacement for Cuban wrapper I had been waiting for? I reserved judgment until I performed the ultimate test. I had a few sample cigars made out of the Cameroon wrapper and smoked them. Anyone within a hundred-yard radius of my office that day must have been jolted by my sudden outburst:

"My God, that's the best tobacco I've ever had outside of Cuba! It's got the taste, it's got the burn, it's got everything we want for the future. This is it!"

I was delighted beyond my wildest expectations. It was surprisingly similar to Cuban tobacco in appearance, but with better burning qualities and an exceptional taste all its own. I had to learn more about this extraordinary tobacco.

The following year, in 1962, I made a trip to the Netherlands to visit Anton van Beck at his home office in Rotterdam. I inspected and sampled the Cameroon wrapper tobacco he had and it was just as good as I remembered. Our supply of Cuban tobacco was running out, and I wanted to acquire as much Cameroon tobacco as I could.

Van Beck was accustomed to dealing with smaller European cigar manufacturers who usually purchased a few bales of tobacco at a time. He was completely taken aback when I told him I was interested in buying at least several hundred bales.

"I'm afraid we couldn't provide even half that much," van Beck said, after recovering his composure. "The most we can get for you is fifty bales."

"I'll take it," I said. Our Cuban supply would tide us over for one more year if we were very careful with it. But next year, I would have to be able to purchase large quantities of Cameroon wrapper. The only way to do that was to buy it at the annual Cameroon Wrapper Inscription, a two-week-long auction held every June in Paris. It was sponsored by the French tobacco monopoly.

The French government had controlled all facets of the tobacco industry in France since the early 1800s. The French tobacco monopoly had been established by none other than Napoleon, the great conqueror to whom my father had so often been compared.

The story goes that Napoleon was attending a reception one day when an attractive woman adorned in expensive jewelry caught his eye. He invited her to dance and learned that her husband was in the tobacco business. Napoleon decided that such an overt display of wealth should not go un-taxed, and formed the French tobacco monopoly to provide an additional source of revenue with which to finance his costly expansionist wars.

Joep Van Huystee samples the bales at the Cameroon Inscription in 1973 while Bobby looks on

Since 1953, cigar manufacturers, tobacco dealers, and brokers from around the world had been coming to Paris every year to buy Cameroon tobacco from the French tobacco monopoly, which ran the Inscription. In June of 1963 I attended my first Cameroon Wrapper Inscription, accompanied by a team from A.L. van Beck as my purchasing agents.

Samples representing thousands of bales of tobacco were displayed in a huge auditorium for the examination of cigar manufacturers and tobacco dealers, with different grades exhibited each day. Each manufacturer had his own small office, where he could inspect random samples of the different grades in private. I often asked to have the samples moistened, which helped to evaluate the tobacco's elasticity and sturdiness. I recorded all my observations into an Inscription notebook.

On the last two days of the Inscription, a series of auctions known as Tempos were held. Different lots of tobacco were auctioned during each Tempo and participants wrote down their offers on sealed bids. The bids grew higher and higher as the Tempos progressed.

What a nerve-wracking way to buy tobacco! In the beginning, I hated it. I couldn't help but second-guess myself. When I won a bid, I wondered whether I could have paid less. When I didn't win, I never knew by how much I had lost. Could I have won the bid if only I had offered a little more?

Examining tobacco wrapper samples at the Cameroon Inscription with George Gershal of Consolidated Cigar, Bernie Seltzer and Tony Regensburg of Bayuk Cigar, and Johnny Gorman of American Cigar

Eventually, I got the hang of it. After attending the Inscription for several years, I even came to enjoy it. It was very much like playing cards: Winning depended upon keeping track of the other players' hands. Over the years, I learned which manufacturers wanted the same type of tobacco I did, and figured out how many bales they normally purchased. When a competitor won a bid on the type of tobacco I wanted in the early Tempos—and had purchased all the bales he needed—then I knew I could bid lower on the next lot of tobacco, because he was no longer in the game.

I also liked the fact that my dollar was just as good as the next fellow's. No matter how big or small a manufacturer you were, everyone was equal in the sealed bid process. At least that had always been the case until 1974.

About a month before the Inscription that year, one of the supervisors in our factory came to see me with some unpleasant news.

"Something strange is going on," he began. "One of our employees was at the Cuban Club last night. He ran into a buddy of his who works for another cigar company here in Tampa and they got to talking. When our employee mentioned that we were getting ready for the Inscription in Paris next month, his friend said his company wasn't going because they had already purchased their Cameroon wrapper from this year's crop."

It turned out that this company had purchased tobacco under the table from a manager of the French tobacco monopoly without going through the Inscription process. This placed all the other cigar manufacturers at a disadvantage. I confronted the Inscription officials with the news that the integrity of the Inscription had been compromised. They tracked down the man responsible and fired him. To apologize for the embarrassment, the Inscription officials hosted a dinner in my honor at Louis Relais XIII, a famous Paris restaurant dating back to the 18th century.

For the first ten years that I attended the Inscription, there was only one other American firm, the American Cigar Company, buying Cameroon tobacco. However, they purchased the darker, less expensive grades to use on their cheaper cigars. We were the first American cigar manufacturer to use Cameroon tobacco for premium cigars.

None of the other U.S. cigar companies wanted to use Cameroon tobacco because it was too expensive. In 1960, the average price for a pound of Cuban wrapper tobacco was

At the Inscription with George Gershal and Johnny Gorman

seven dollars. Cameroon wrapper had been about the same price, but soon after the embargo, it skyrocketed to fourteen dollars a pound. None of the other American companies were willing to pay that.

I believed it was worth the cost. As my father always told me, if you make and sell something of quality, you can stay in business for a hundred years. If you make and sell something on the basis of price, someone else can always make it cheaper, and you can be out of business in six months.

I was obsessed with using only the finest quality tobacco, regardless of price. My philosophy was that if you paid too much for good tobacco, you only lost your money. If you paid too much for poor tobacco, you lost your money *and* your customers.

One year, when the Cameroon tobacco crop was in short supply, I set an Inscription record for the highest bid ever offered in the auction's history. I joked that if one of my employees had paid that price, I would have fired him. If I had been working as a tobacco buyer for someone else, I'm sure they would have fired me too.

I believed that if we had the highest quality tobacco, our cigars would sell; that the bitterness of poor quality remains in a smoker's mouth long after the sweetness of low price is forgotten. And I was right.

Our premium cigar business went through a period of substantial growth because no one else was using Cameroon wrapper. I used Cameroon wrapper in combination with Central American filler and Connecticut binder for our Cuesta-Rey cigars. We copyrighted the term "ACW," for African Cameroon Wrapper, and promoted it on our Cuesta-Rey packaging. Cameroon tobacco propelled our company to the next level, and in the 1960s, Cuesta-Rey rose to prominence as one of the top-selling premium cigars in the country.

For twenty-five years, I spent two weeks every June at the tobacco Inscription in Paris. It was an exhausting process and very hard work, leaving little time for sightseeing. I always looked forward to the end of the day when we would go out for dinner with our Inscription team at one of the many wonderful Parisian restaurants. I often brought Elaine with me to Paris and we would visit the cathedrals and artist colonies on weekends.

My annual pilgrimages to Paris also gave me the opportunity to learn more about the European cigar industry. I toured cigar factories throughout the continent, in Sweden, Belgium, Switzerland, the Netherlands, Germany, and England. I loved the packaging I found in these countries. In general, it was more attractive than what we had in America: the colors were more vivid, the designs more elegant, and the materials simply of a finer quality. I began to incorporate European styles of packaging for our cigars.

In 1964, the Surgeon General issued a report on the health hazards associated with cigarette smoking. Obviously, the report was bad news for cigarette manufacturers, but it gave a dramatic boost to cigar sales, as many cigarette smokers switched to cigars. The number of cigars produced in 1964 reached nine billion, the highest it had been since World War II.

However, the good news for cigar manufacturers did not last long. From that 1964 peak, cigar sales fell steadily by three to five percent a year for nearly three decades.

The years ahead presented extraordinary difficulties, but I faced them with the understanding that behind every challenge lies an opportunity.

How's business at M & N?

GREAT, thank you!

Cuesta-Rey and Rigoletto Cigars have broken all sales records during 1964 . . .

Thanks to your help!

Millard Newman

"The year 1964 has been the biggest year in our long history. We have concentrated our efforts on producing a fine, premium quality cigar . . . a cigar that neatly blends mildness, smoothness and rich bouquet into the most satisfying smoke in the world.

"You have 'spread their fame', and made Cuesta-Rey and Rigoletto two of America's fastest selling top brands.

"As we begin 1965, we are ready with the most hard-hitting, consistent advertising program ever to appear in major newspapers and national magazines on our brands.

"Attractive packages, handsomely designed to help you sell have been prepared . . . and as always, our uniform, high quality will continue to be our trademark.

"We are going to work with you again in 1965, Mr. Dealer, in every way we can, just as you have with us, to acquaint millions more smokers with the premium quality of Cuesta-Rey and Rigoletto Cigars . . . made in Tampa."

Millard Newman
President

M & N Cigar Manufacturers, Inc.
TAMPA, FLORIDA
Manufacturers of Premium Quality Cigars Since 1895

A very good year

Why is Cuesta-Rey #95 America's largest selling 75¢ cigar?

ANSWER:

- Made of all Natural Leaf tobacco
- Made of selected imported long leaf filler.
- Rolled with aged rare Cameroon English Market Selection Wrapper (ACW*)*
- Skillfully crafted in Tampa by cigar makers in the same tradition of quality since 1884.
- Hand packed with aged cedar in natural wood cabinets.

- Also hand packed in gold and black packets of 3 cigars with exclusive polyethylene liners to assure long lasting factory freshness.
- Choice of smokers who are accustomed to the taste and aroma of fine imported leaf.

Send for the special offer today so you too can soon enjoy the fine quality CUESTA-REY #95 cigar.

*African Cameroon Wrappers

'95 English Market Selection

SPECIAL OFFER | **CUESTA-REY**
ALL NATURAL LEAF CIGARS

The Cuesta-Rey No. 95 free offer

One of our most significant challenges was the self-service phenomenon that had swept through retailing in the 1950s and now finally caught on in the cigar business in the early 1960s. Retailers had traditionally sold cigars individually from boxes in humidified display cases. Suddenly, the humidor cases disappeared, as large retailers replaced them with self-service display racks. For the first time, cigars were being sold in cardboard packs of three, four, or five cigars, rather than individually from a display box. Humidification, as every cigar lover knows, is critical to protect cigars from drying out. Shelf life became a major concern.

I began experimenting with different types of protective wrapping material that would keep our cigars in factory-fresh condition without the benefit of outside humidification. DuPont Chemical laboratories conducted tests for us and confirmed that polyethylene provided a superior moisture barrier for maximum shelf life. I discovered that placing cigars in a polyethylene pouch that was double-folded at the top kept them fresh for a full year.

Having developed a better method of protecting cigars, I drew on the lessons I had learned in Europe to come up with a superior outer packaging. We designed a humidor pack with laminated, brushed gold foil that distinguished Cuesta-Rey from the multitude of new cigar packs entering the market. As far as I know, no other American cigar manufacturer was using this foil packaging at the time, and it certainly helped Cuesta-Rey catch the consumer's eye.

Advertising also played an important part in my campaign to establish Cuesta-Rey as the leading premium cigar in America. I was visiting the cosmetics counter at Bloomingdale's in New York when I came up with an idea that transformed our entire advertising strategy. I have always enjoyed looking at cosmetics counters in department stores because I admire the beautiful packaging of cosmetics and fragrances. Truth be told, I also admire the beautiful women behind the counter.

On this particular trip to Bloomingdale's, I overheard a gentleman ask for a bottle of Chanel No. 19. This surprised me, as I had only ever heard of Chanel No. 5. Intrigued, I asked the salesclerk to explain.

"Our advertising focuses exclusively on Chanel No. 5," she said. "We piggyback all our other items on top of that."

I thought this was a terrific idea. One of the things that had been bothering me for some time was the fact that we were advertising so many different cigar sizes. Now I knew this was unnecessary. When I returned to Tampa I told my brother that we should take all of the money we had to spend on advertising and spend it on one cigar: Cuesta-Rey No. 95. Zeroing in on one flagship brand worked very well for us.

We developed one special offer whereby consumers could get a free sample pack of Cuesta-Rey No. 95 cigars packaged in a small redwood box we called the "Traveling Man's Humidor." We advertised this program in every major newspaper in America, as well as in leading magazines like *Time, Newsweek, Forbes, Sports Illustrated,* and the *New York Times Magazine.*

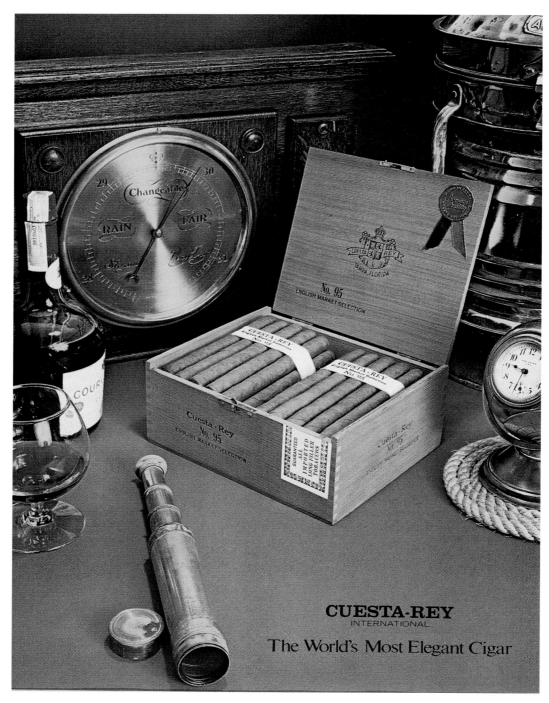

A Cuesta-Rey advertisement

Because of these innovations in manufacturing (Cameroon wrapper), packaging (gold foil), marketing (sampling), and advertising, by the mid-1960s, Cuesta-Rey had become one of America's top-selling premium cigars.

We maintained our position in the marketplace by continually coming out with new shapes and sizes. In 1960, we introduced St. Regis, one of the industry's first little cigars. St. Regis was also notable as the first cigar to use homogenized tobacco for the wrapper. Our advertising agency came up with a catchy jingle to promote St. Regis that was played on radio stations all over the country. I can still sing the tune.

The 1960s saw many cigar manufacturers stepping up their production of little cigars, but by 1970, I felt that the trend had peaked. While the whole cigar industry was still focused on thin cigars to appeal to younger people, I was thinking about thick cigars. I didn't want young smokers. I wanted to capture the market of middle-aged cigar lovers who appreciated traditional, thicker cigars.

In 1971, I decided to introduce a thick cigar called Rigoletto Black Jack, a maduro cigar with a dark, flavorsome wrapper and a ring gauge of forty-seven. (The ring gauge measures 1/64th of an inch and is the standard measurement of a cigar's thickness.) A forty-seven-ring gauge was exceptionally thick compared to most cigars on the market at the time. I had wanted to introduce a black tobacco cigar with the name of Black Jack for some time, having registered the Black Jack label with the U.S. Patent Office several years earlier.

My decision to introduce a thick cigar met with some opposition within our company. My nephew, Bill, who was working with his father, Millard, in our sales department, thought Rigoletto Black Jack would never sell. He felt that since our competitors were all coming out with thin cigars, we should do the same. I held to my belief that we would never be successful by copying our competitors. We had to do something original. As I had anticipated, Rigoletto Black Jack sold extremely well. It remains our best-selling Tampa-made cigar to this day.

My philosophy throughout the 1960s and '70s was that although we were relatively small compared to the big northern cigar companies, and operating in a somewhat shrinking market, there would always be a certain number of cigars consumed. If we were clever enough, we could get a bigger share of that market. And that's just what happened.

My only regret was that my father wasn't around to see it.

CIGAR FAMILY

CHANGING OF THE GUARD

*W*hile I certainly encouraged my sons to join the family business, I never pressured them into it. It was their decision. All I asked of them was to do their best in whatever field they chose.

Bobby seemed to choose the cigar business at an early age. I had taken my sons to visit our factory, usually on Saturdays when we worked half-days, ever since they were little boys. One such Saturday afternoon, I was working at the partner's desk I shared with my brother, Millard, when Bobby piped up: "Someday, Eric and I are going to sit just like that!"

What clinched it for Bobby was a family vacation we took in 1961 when he was ten years old. Elaine and I had taken our sons to Miami Beach for the Labor Day weekend. Wherever I travel, I like to visit the local tobacconists, and I had taken Bobby with me on some of my rounds. I was talking with the owner of one of the Miami smokeshops when a customer came in and bought a pack of Rigoletto Palma Grandes. Just the week before, Bobby had seen these same cigars being made at our factory in Tampa. He recognized the deep, royal blue of the packaging, which I had chosen because of its similarity to the blue on the McCormick pepper package, a color I had always admired. Bobby was amazed to see the cigars made in his father's factory being sold here in Miami Beach. It left quite an impression, and I think he was hooked on the cigar business from that moment on.

During their college years, Eric and Bobby spent their summer vacations working with our salesmen and tobacco distributors selling Cuesta-Rey and Rigoletto, and from 1970, they accompanied me to the annual Cameroon Inscriptions in Paris, where they learned how tobacco was sold.

When they first started working with me, they couldn't believe what they saw. At home I was a pussycat: docile, easygoing, never angry. At work, I was quite the opposite: focused, intense, not much smile, and very, very serious. They told me it was like I flipped a switch when I came to work. They started calling me Dr. Jeckyl and Mr. Hyde. My wife joked that she was glad she lived with Dr. Jeckyl.

Eric attended the University of the South in Sewanee, Tennessee, and played football all four years. As a freshman, he just got beaten to a pulp. He was smaller than most of the other players, but he was fast, and by his sophomore year became a first-team defensive guard. I was proud of him, although I was never too keen on his playing football. It seemed wacky to risk getting his brains knocked out.

In the second game of his senior year, he tackled a running back so hard that Eric suffered a seizure and was hospitalized for several days. He had such a bad concussion that he didn't know where he was. He completely recovered, but because of his injury, Eric, who

Eric at only 170 pounds, a starting defensive guard at Sewanee

was enrolled in the Air Force ROTC, was reclassified as 4F: not qualified to serve. With one swift kick, both his football and military careers were ended.

After graduating from Sewanee in 1970, Eric went on to earn his MBA from Emory University in Atlanta. Elaine and I encouraged him to continue on to law school or perhaps pursue a doctoral degree, but he decided against it. "I like business," he told us, "and as long as I have a cigar business to go into, why shouldn't I?"

Eric's decision to join M & N was greatly influenced by his sense of fairness. He felt that since he had a spot waiting for him at M & N, taking a position at another company would be depriving someone else of a job. "Why would I take somebody else's place, someone that might really need the job?" he said.

Bobby sets a Florida state record for the discus

At first, Eric wasn't so fond of the cigar business, but he grew to enjoy it as he went along, much as I had back in the 1930s. Eric spent his first year at the company working in the factory, spending about eight weeks in each department. After eight weeks in the cigar-making department, he was making 3,500 cigars a day—not as much as the more experienced cigarmakers, but not bad for a recent college grad. Eric naturally gravitated toward the manufacturing and marketing side of things. He developed some wonderful efficiency programs for the factory and took on the responsibility for the development and procurement of our packaging.

Bobby joined the company in 1975 after receiving his bachelor's degree from Sewanee and his MBA from Tulane University in New Orleans. Bobby concentrated on the sales side of the business, working with my brother and his son, Bill, to expand Cuesta-Rey and

Golfing together in the Grand Bahamas in August 1963

CIGAR FAMILY

Rigoletto distribution. Bobby devoted most of his energy to the Southeastern market, where Eli Witt was still our key distributor.

While working in the Nashville market, Bobby met an Eli Witt salesman named Bobby Knox whom he thought was just terrific. He had been working for Eli Witt for twenty-four years, since he was nineteen years old, and was looking to make a change. Bobby urged Millard and me to hire him, and after a lot of arm-twisting to overcome Millard's reluctance, Bobby Knox became our Southeastern sales manager in 1977. The two Bobbys made a terrific team, and together they dramatically increased our sales in the Southeast.

My sons had entered the business at a time when the industry as a whole was steadily declining. We managed to buck the trend. Staying alive in the cigar business in the 1970s took a great deal of ingenuity. You had to come out with new brands, new packages, new promotions, new ideas. While most cigar companies saw their businesses decreasing, our share of the market was increasing, in part because of all the effort I had put into building our brands in the 1960s.

By 1970, Cuesta-Rey had become the leading premium cigar brand in retail stores in the United States. Always looking for ways to expand our distribution into new markets, I hit upon the idea of selling Cuesta-Rey in restaurants. Many restaurants still permitted cigar smoking in the 1970s, although they were not in the practice of selling cigars. The centerpiece of my campaign to put restaurants in the cigar business was a handsome mahogany humidor that we offered free with the purchase of an assortment of Cuesta-Rey premium cigars. The restaurants kept our humidors on display in their establishments and simply ordered refills as the cigars sold out. I could not have anticipated how well this would turn out: Our Cuesta-Rey Ambassador Cabinet was soon being carried in some 20,000 restaurants.

Business was still good through the late 1970s. It wasn't until the early 1980s that the decline caught up with us, brought on by a new source of competition looming on the horizon.

I saw it coming as early as 1970: Cuban cigarmakers who had fled to Nicaragua, Honduras, Ecuador, and the Dominican Republic after Castro took power had slowly but steadily cultivated new tobacco plantations and had begun making cigars by hand in their adopted countries. Many of them had brought Cuban seeds with them, growing tobacco that was, if not identical to that grown on Cuban soil, often almost as good.

This new cottage industry was comprised mostly of small, humble, family-owned operations. These manufacturers could make larger and cheaper cigars by hand than we could by machine in Tampa, since their labor costs were lower and our machines were limited to producing certain sizes.

One of these new offshore manufacturers was the renowned Menendez and Garcia family of Havana, the original producers of the famous Cuban Montecristo and H. Upmann brands, who had set up shop in the Canary Islands. By the late sixties, Menendez and Garcia's new Montecruz brand—the name was probably as close as they could get to the original Montecristo name without encountering trademark problems with Cuba—was at the forefront of a growing imported handmade cigar market in the U.S. Montecruz was but the first of many imported handmade cigar brands that began making inroads in some of our key markets, including Cleveland, Detroit, Chicago, Los Angeles, and New York.

We were still successful selling machine-made cigars throughout the sixties and seventies, because Cuesta-Rey was so well known. But by the early 1980s, our machine-made business was eroding on a daily basis. Our fellow cigar manufacturers in Tampa were hit even harder than we were by the erosion of the machine-made cigar business. It got to the point where the vast majority of cigar smokers only desired imported handmade cigars. Who wanted to buy a machine-made cigar when you could get a much larger, hand-rolled cigar for the same price?

I knew we had to get involved in the imported handmade cigar business. Finding the right offshore manufacturing partner was critical. I discussed this with my brother at length. We considered a number of different cigar manufacturers from Nicaragua and Honduras to make Cuesta-Rey, but I never felt comfortable with any of them.

"They don't have the background, they don't have the facilities, and they don't know what good tobacco is. They can't make good cigars." I told Millard.

My brother was peeved: "You know, if we don't get into the handmade cigar business soon, we're not going to be in business at all. We're losing market share all over the country, especially in New York."

In the early 1980s, Cuesta-Rey still had a certain momentum in New York, a critical market, but it was practically the only machine-made cigar that was still selling there. I knew that eventually we would not be able to sell any premium cigars unless they were made by hand.

"I am well aware of the situation," I said. "But I have to find someone I can trust completely, someone I know has the same experience and passion for cigars that I have. Otherwise, I might as well start a factory in Latin America myself." I seriously considered doing just that, but it would necessarily be a last resort.

As our business continued to slide, people in my family suggested we diversify.

"Why don't we get into another line of business?" they would say.

My reply was always the same: "Because I know the cigar business. What do I know about any other industry? I don't know anybody's business but my own."

Elaine and I still connecting with politics in the 1970s, here with First Lady Rosalyn Carter and Florida Governor (now Senator) Bob Graham

Family tensions within the company were mounting. Statistically, less than one percent of family businesses ever last for three or more generations. And I know why from first-hand experience. When you've got troubles with your relatives, you've got real troubles.

We now had a total of fourteen relatives, including myself, who owned shares of the company, all of them collecting dividends and making demands for more. Making decisions of any importance required time-consuming board meetings in which little was accomplished. It was as if we were a public company: Our relatives were stockholders, always asking for more dividends, trying to take capital out when we needed the money for daily operations. The entire cigar industry was in a terrible slump. Our profits were shrinking, and with new family members coming into the business, there was less and less to go around.

On top of that, there were philosophical differences between us. Too many of my relatives simply had no enthusiasm for cigars. One of them compared the cigar business to the buggy whip business: a dying industry with no future. How can you possibly succeed with an attitude like that?

The family disagreed about almost everything. The one thing we all agreed on was that something had to change.

At the beginning of 1986, I decided to take charge of the situation. The cigar industry was in decline. Our company profits were shrinking. And nothing was being done about it because our company shareholders could not agree on a course of action. Someone had to put an end to our family squabbling once and for all. My brother and I had gotten along fine when it was just the two of us, but now that both of our families were involved in the business, it just didn't work. We could no longer run the company together. Only one of us could sit on the throne. One of us had to buy the other one out.

I walked into Millard's office and laid my cards on the table.

"Our business cannot continue the way it's been going," I said. "One of us should get out of this business."

Millard knew just as well as I that something had to give.

"I want to buy you out," I continued. "How much do you want for your shares in the company?"

Millard quoted a ridiculously high figure. It was twice as much as I believed the company was worth.

"You know the net worth of this company," I said. "And you want twice as much for it? That's not right. A realistic figure is half as much."

"Well," Millard replied. "If you want to buy the business, that's what you've got to pay me."

"I'll tell you what," I said. "If you can raise fifty percent of what you just quoted, then *you* can buy *me* out. I'll give you six weeks. At the end of that time, if you haven't been able to come up with the money, then *I'll* buy *you* out for the same amount."

I honestly didn't know how it was going to play out. All I knew was that one of us had to get out of the business. At that point, I didn't care whether it was him or me.

Six weeks later, the day of reckoning arrived. I honestly thought Millard was going to get the company. I was wrong.

"You've got the business," Millard said.

"What happened?"

"I couldn't raise the financing. The banks were only willing to loan me the money if I agreed to put up my Rolls Royce collection as collateral. My auto collection is like my children. You know I can't do that."

Millard's fascination with automobiles, which began back in the Depression, had blossomed over the years into a serious pastime of collecting antique Rolls Royces. He now owned at least ten of them, all very rare models, some of which dated back to 1903. He had restored most of them himself.

"The company is yours if you can come up with the money," he said.

My brother thought I would never be able to raise the money. Millard's thinking was that if he couldn't do it, neither could I. In fact, I had already figured out how to obtain the financing, in part by mortgaging our factory building. But he didn't know that. Millard believed that when all was said and done, he would end up running the company.

It was during this time, in January of 1986, that our annual sales meeting was scheduled to take place. Thinking he would be running the company after I failed to buy him out, Millard did not want to spend the money to bring all of our salesmen to Tampa. I insisted that the meeting was absolutely necessary. Millard insisted it was a waste of money. My brother went so far as to consult an attorney, who advised him to demand $50,000 from me in exchange for his permission to go ahead with the sales meeting.

"If you want the sales meeting, I want $50,000 from you personally or the deal is off," Millard told me. If I didn't give him the money, he would not allow me to acquire his shares of the company.

"Okay," I said. "This is what I will do. I will compromise and give you half in cash, tomorrow."

I wrote him a letter spelling out the agreement: I would give him $25,000 in cash. If the deal went through, we would deduct the $25,000 from the purchase price of his stock. If the deal did not go through, he would keep the $25,000. Millard agreed.

Shortly thereafter, and much to my brother's surprise, I came up with the financing. I used the proceeds from mortgaging our factory to redeem his shares in the company. Millard was no longer a shareholder of M & N Cigar Manufacturers. I thought I would now own two-thirds of the company. After all, I had owned a third of the company before purchasing Millard's third. That left my relatives up north, who owned the last third.

I soon discovered that as logical as that may sound, it didn't work that way. Because I had redeemed my brother's shares through the company, the structure of ownership had changed. Now there were two major shareholders instead of three. I now owned half of the company, not two-thirds, and my other relatives owned the other half.

My relatives up north realized this too. When they heard that I was buying out my brother, they called me with some unpleasant, but not entirely unexpected news. The gist of it was: "We're coming down to Tampa to be your partners!"

This was unthinkable. I went to bed that night trying to figure out how I could prevent this from happening. I woke up in a sweat. The only way to do it was to buy them out too. I called my relatives and told them I was prepared to buy their shares of the company. They informed me that they would be willing to sell for the same amount I paid Millard. In strictly business terms, their stock had the same value as Millard's. It was only fair that I pay them the same.

But how was I going to come up with the money? Fortunately, I had a lot of experience dealing with banks. By its very nature, the cigar business requires a great deal of financing. There's a slow turnover on inventory (the tobacco) and a slow return on your investment, so you rely on creditors to help finance your tobacco purchases. I had always been interested in the financial side of the business and over the years, had developed some good

With my brother, Millard

relationships with various banks. In fact, one of Tampa's leading bankers, Lee Bentley, was a good friend of mine; a mentor, really. Lee had helped me become a founding director of the Second National Bank of Tampa, which was later sold to the First National Bank of Tampa, and I had served on their boards for many years. I even considered setting up my own investment firm if the buyout of my relatives didn't go through.

In the end, it didn't make much difference that I had good connections in the Tampa banking community. I still needed to borrow a lot of money. No bank just gives it away. And this was several million dollars.

I had to give up a lot of assets, borrow personally, and mortgage my house. Naturally, I had to get Elaine's blessing. She always ran the household, but when it came to business decisions, she ceded to my judgment. She said she trusted me and agreed to put up the house as collateral.

On February 14—Valentine's Day—1986, my sons and I sat down with all the shareholders around the conference table at our attorney's office and signed our lives away. I was taking a huge risk. At the age of 70, when most people have already retired, I was mortgaging most of my assets. I could have backed out of the deal, but I had every confidence in my sons and myself that we would be successful. I knew we were doing the right thing. If for some reason things didn't work out, I figured I could always live on social security. However, I never believed it would come to that. My relatives got the money and my sons and I got the debt, but we also got the opportunity to turn the company around.

Although my relatives put me through the ringer on the buyout, I couldn't stay angry with them. If our roles had been reversed, I would not have treated them the way they treated me, but I don't hold grudges. To show them that I wanted to put the past behind us, I invited all my relatives to dinner that very Valentine's Day evening. I was extending an olive branch, saying, in effect, let's bury the hatchet; we're still family.

It wasn't the most relaxed dinner I've ever had—tensions were high—but everyone at least made an attempt at civility. In a small way, I think it helped put us all on the path toward reconciliation. I'm happy to say that in the years that followed, we all got along much better. Now that we're no longer partners, it's much easier to enjoy each other purely as family.

My sister Helen's son, Richard Schanfarber, who inherited Helen's shares in M & N when she died in 1985, treated us the same way after the buyout as before—with friendship and respect. My sister Elaine's husband, Al Rogan, who did so much for us in Michigan during our national expansion after World War II, stayed with the company as an employee until he retired in 1992, and he was a real asset. Elaine herself was pleased to see me continue our father's legacy.

The day after the buyout, I drove to our factory very early in the morning before anyone else arrived. I wanted some time alone to savor the moment. Yesterday, my sons and I had owned thirty-three percent. Today, we owned all of it—lock, stock, and barrel. Eric became president; Bobby, executive vice president of sales and marketing. I became Chairman of the Board. What a proud day. When my sons arrived, they found me standing at the entrance of the factory—*our* factory—soaking it all in.

"Just look at it!" I said. "It's all ours. Just the three of us. Doesn't that feel good?"

Ever the pragmatist, Eric waited only a moment before replying: "We don't own it, Dad. The banks own it."

Indeed they did, or would soon enough if we failed to turn the business around. We were highly leveraged, having traded our assets for bank debt to attain ownership of the company.

Father and sons

We no longer had relatives for partners: We had banks for partners, and it's no fun trying to build your business with a bunch of nervous bankers breathing down your neck.

It was bad enough having bankers for partners, but that was heaven compared to having the government as a partner. The financial institution with whom we mortgaged our factory was a Savings and Loan. By the late 1980s, the S & L industry was losing billions of dollars due to rampant fraud and bad investments made after Congress deregulated the industry in 1982. By early 1989, about one in six Savings and Loans was bankrupt. Our S & L went belly-up along with the rest of them. In August of 1989, Congress passed a bill creating the

Resolution Trust Corporation to dispose of ailing S & Ls and transfer their assets to new institutions as part of a multi-billion-dollar bailout.

All of a sudden we had a new partner: The Resolution Trust Corporation, and they were not lenders—they were liquidators. We also had loans with regular commercial banks, which were under the gun as well. The government was closely monitoring their activities because they did not want what happened to the Savings and Loan industry to happen to the commercial banking industry.

It was a challenging time for us. The difficulties of being highly leveraged were only compounded by the continuing decline of the cigar industry. However, I always believed that sooner or later, things would work out. There are always challenges to overcome. But if you dwell on the negatives, you can't stay in business.

I am an optimist at heart, just like my father, and I never lost faith in myself or my sons. Together, we made it through these difficult times and emerged stronger than ever.

SMOKE DREAMS COME TRUE

*T*he turning point that set us on the path to becoming a prominent force in the premium handmade cigar business occurred just three weeks after our Valentine's Day buyout in 1986. It was the day Carlos Fuente showed up at my office with a business proposition that changed our lives forever.

I had known Carlos Fuente for a long time. He was a fellow Tampa cigar manufacturer and we had become acquainted shortly after I moved to Tampa. Like the Cuestas, the Fuente family had an impressive history in the cigar business. After the Spanish-American War, Carlos's father, Arturo Fuente Sr., moved from his home in Cuba to West Tampa, where he founded the Arturo Fuente Cigar Company in 1912. The Fuente business was very much a family affair. Every day after school, Arturo's sons, Carlos and Arturo, Jr., were expected to roll fifty cigars before they could go out and play. Carlos took over the company in 1960 and persevered through some very tough times.

Carlos is my kind of guy: passionate about cigars, uncompromising in the quality of his product, and possessed of an incredible work ethic. He is in a league by himself, a true visionary and the brightest fellow you would ever want to know. Besides being one of the best cigar manufacturers in the world, he is also an artist, a mechanic, and an architect. He is a hands-on perfectionist, never satisfied with the status quo, always trying to make things better. Carlos has the same philosophy as I have: He believes quality will always win out in the end. He consistently invested his profits into increasing his tobacco inventory, ensuring that it will be properly aged. All told, he is an incredible person who truly pulled himself up by his bootstraps.

Over time, Carlos built Arturo Fuente into a fairly successful Tampa brand. To compete more effectively in the growing imported handmade cigar category, Carlos opened a second cigar factory in Nicaragua in 1976. Tragically, his factory burned down during the Samosa uprisings. Not to be discouraged, he established a new operation in Honduras. Incredibly, this second factory met a similar fate. Carlos was not one to give up in the face of adversity. In 1980, he opened another cigar factory in Santiago in the Dominican Republic.

Meanwhile, Carlos's son, Carlos Jr., continued to oversee the Fuentes' Tampa operation. By the mid-1980s, their handmade business in the Dominican Republic was really taking off, while their machine-made business was in decline like everyone else's. It was under these circumstances that Carlos Fuente Sr. came to visit me in March 1986. After we inquired about each other's families and exchanged a few pleasantries, he came to the reason for his visit.

"Stanford, I would like to close my factory here in Tampa. I would rather not eliminate our machine-made business entirely, and I was wondering if you would consider making our Tampa machine-made cigars for us."

Carlos showed me the prices he was getting for his machine-made cigars and I quickly estimated how much it would cost us to make them.

With my friend, Carlos Fuente

"Carlos, I can't make a profit on this," I said. "But I'll tell you what. I don't care if I make anything. I'll make these cigars for you, but I want you to do me a favor in return. The only person in this whole world that I would trust to make imported cigars for us is you. I've looked and looked for people to make handmade cigars and I haven't found anyone that I'm satisfied with. Will you make some for us?"

"Sure I will," Carlos said.

"This is what I want to do. We have a brand named La Unica that I acquired from Karl Cuesta. I'm not doing anything with it, but I like the brand. I don't know the handmade market nearly as well as you, so how about if you select the four shapes that you think would sell the best. Then let's come up with a tobacco blend that we both like."

I went on to explain that I wanted to sell La Unica in bundles instead of boxes. By eliminating the cost of boxes, we could offer a higher quality cigar and pass the savings on to the consumer at lower prices. However, I didn't like any of the bundled cigars on the market at that time. Most of them were "factory seconds" made from scraps of leftover tobacco, usually by inexperienced trainees, and inferior in quality.

"The only way I know how to do this is for you to make high-quality cigars. All the other bundled brands are seconds, so let's sell La Unica as firsts, and put the Spanish word Primeros on the label. That way, everyone can tell these are premium cigars. We'll place them in 300 stores for six months and see how it goes."

When we introduced La Unica Dominican Primeros in the summer of 1986, it was the first premium cigar ever sold in bundles. We chose to use Dominican filler and binder with Connecticut wrapper in both natural and maduro. Selling La Unica took some doing because it was more expensive than any other bundled cigar on the market. I trusted that consumers would pay the higher price once they realized it was a better smoke.

Shortly after we began introducing La Unica, my son, Bobby, called me from Houston to tell me he had just sold his first big order to a chain of ten smokeshops.

"This fellow really likes La Unica," Bobby said. "He gave me an order for 10,000 cigars! There's just one thing. He doesn't want to use the La Unica name. He wants us to put his own label on them."

"Well, Bobby," I said, "we're not only selling cigars; we're selling *brands*. If we sell him La Unica and he puts his own name on it, we haven't really sold anything. You go back and tell him to ask General Cigar Company if they would be willing to put his name on their Macanudos."

General Cigar would not even consider selling a brand as popular as Macanudo under someone else's name, although there were plenty of smaller cigar manufacturers who were happy to make private labels. It's an easy way to sell cigars, but a dead end in the long run.

You have no equity when you make private label cigars. Your customer can always find someone else to make them cheaper. Then you've lost the business. Real equity comes from manufacturing your own brands. No one else can make a Cuesta-Rey cigar. People have to come to us to get it.

Bobby went back to the man in Houston and explained our position. If he wanted our cigars, he would have to take them with the La Unica name. He declined. When Bobby told me what had happened, I told him not to worry. "That's okay, Bobby. Go sell to somebody else in the area."

Six months later, La Unica had become so popular in Houston that the retailer changed his mind and placed an order. To this day, La Unica remains the best-selling premium bundled cigar in America.

In recent years, I heard an amusing story about a superstar athlete who signed an endorsement deal with one of our competitors. As part of the deal, he received free boxes of cigars every month. Apparently, he didn't care for them too much, because he showed up at Coffman's Tobacco Shop in Stuart, Florida, one day with ten boxes of them under his arm, asking the tobacconist, Susan Griggs, if he could exchange them for bundles of La Unica. Now that's brand equity. Susan said no and telephoned our competitor's home office to complain that their endorsement deal had cost her a good customer.

I was so pleased with La Unica's success that I asked Carlos Fuente to start making Cuesta-Rey cigars for us. We began with a new size of Cuesta-Rey named 1884 after the year the brand was founded. We introduced Cuesta-Rey 1884 in three-packs of natural and maduro. A premium handmade cigar priced at one dollar—it did exceptionally well.

I ultimately decided to transfer all of our Cuesta-Rey premium cigar sizes to the Fuente factory. The first of these was our flagship brand, Cuesta-Rey No. 95. By 1991, all of our

Cuesta-Rey cigars were being handmade in the Dominican Republic. Although many cigar brands made the transition from handmade to machine-made, Cuesta-Rey is one of the few that ever completed the circle and went back to being handmade.

In 1990, we embarked on a new venture with the Fuentes. One of my father's philosophies for success had been to build our own sales organization. He believed in controlling our own destiny by controlling our own distribution, rather than relying on brokers to represent our products. We now had one of the top sales and distribution organizations in the country, but it was not being used to its full capacity. At the same time, the Fuentes did not have their own salesmen. Fred Zaniboni, Carlos Fuente's sales director, had assembled a superb network of brokers to sell Arturo Fuente cigars, but by their very nature, brokers are independent contractors who represent an assortment of products.

On November 1, 1990, our sales organization began selling and distributing Fuente cigars through a new alliance called FANCO, renamed Fuente & Newman Premium Cigars Ltd. in 1995. From the very beginning, the arrangement worked like magic. We placed Arturo Fuente cigars in hundreds of new smokeshops within the first year of our joint venture.

Eric with Carlos Fuente, father and son

THE TAMPA TRIBUNE

Tampa, Florida, Saturday, October 27, 1990

Business & Finance

BUSINESS & FINANCE

Growing smoke: Two Tampa manufacturers, M&N Cigar Manufacturers Ltd. and Fuente Cigar Ltd., will form a joint nationwide cigar marketing and distribution network. **1D**

2 family-owned cigar makers light up marketing venture

By BILL SHELTON
Tribune Staff Writer

TAMPA — M&N Cigar Manufacturers Inc. and Fuente Cigar Ltd. have organized a cigar distribution company based in Ybor City, company officials announced Friday.

The companies, two of the oldest cigar manufacturers in Tampa, beginning Nov. 1 will operate the joint venture called FANCO from the M&N headquarters at 2701 16th St., said Eric Newman, president of M&N.

The joint venture is important because it marks the first time two Tampa family-owned cigar manufacturers have joined forces to market and distribute cigars, Newman said.

FANCO, which stands for "Fuente and Newman Co.," will give Fuente access to M&N's nationwide marketing and distribution network while improving productivity for M&N's underutilized marketing organization.

"Fuente is very strong in producing top quality cigars, and we are very strong in marketing and distribution," Newman said. "It's a deal that makes a lot of sense."

The new venture was expected to create no new jobs, but strengthen both companies' sales

Tribune photograph by DAVID KADLUBOWSKI
Carlos Fuente, left, and Standford Newman, stand in front of the Standard Cigar Co. factory in Ybor City.

figures, officials said. The companies would not release sales figures.

While the cigar industry nationwide has suffered from weak sales, both M&N and Fuente have remained profitable with brisk sales of the hand-rolled, high-priced, imported cigars, Newman said.

Standard Cigar Co. and Fuente produce the so-called "top premium" hand-rolled imported cigars that each sell for $1 or more.

Except for a few tiny tourist attractions in Ybor City, Tampa manufacturers no longer produce hand-rolled cigars. Several companies still make mass produced machine-made cigars, however.

The two companies have been closely tied since 1986, when Fuente closed its Tampa factory and moved its manufacturing operations to the Dominican Republic, said Carlos Fuente, chairman of Fuente Cigar Ltd.

M&N's premium hand-rolled cigars, the Cuesta-Rey and La Unica brands, are both manufactured by Fuente. Fuente manufactures its own Arturo Fuente and Montesino premium brands.

See CIGAR, Page 8D

Cigar makers join forces for distribution

■ From Page 1D

M&N manufactures the Rigoletto, with prices ranging from 30 cents to 55 cents, with machines at the Ybor factory. M&N also produces for Fuente medium-priced machine-made cigars called the Moya.

"It's a natural alliance," said Stanford Newman, chairman of M&N and Eric Newman's father. "Our La Unica is the largest selling premium hand-made bundle cigar in America and Fuente . . . is now the largest hand-made cigar production operation in the Dominican Republic."

Fuente operates two large factories and employs about 600 people in the Dominican Republic. M&N employs about 150 people in Tampa.

Under the agreement, Stanford Newman will be FANCO's chairman, with Eric Newman president and his brother Robert Newman vice president of sales. Cynthia Fuente Suarez, Carlos Fuente's daughter, will be FANCO's vice president of administration.

FANCO
(today Fuente and Newman Premium Cigars Ltd.)
is formed

Selling cigars for the Fuentes while they made cigars for us proved to be a winning combination that raised both of our businesses to new levels. Having us as one of his biggest customers helped Carlos operate his factory more efficiently, buy better tobacco, and concentrate on what he does best: making the best cigars in the world. By the same token, selling the prestigious Arturo Fuente brand alongside Cuesta-Rey and La Unica gave us a great advantage over our competitors, making each sales call more productive.

Carlos Fuente never wanted to be the biggest, just the best. Ironically, by becoming the best, he also became one of the biggest. With his son, Carlos, Jr., his daughter, Cynthia, and her husband, Wayne Suarez, the Fuente family has become one of the largest, most successful cigar manufacturers in the Dominican Republic. They operate five factories and a beautiful farm outside Santiago named Chateau de la Fuente, where they grow tobacco for their most acclaimed cigars.

I recently looked through my passports and calculated that I have visited the Dominican Republic thirty-seven times since 1986. Every time I visit the Fuente operation, I am impressed by how much they have accomplished since my last visit.

Today, the Fuente family is the most famous in the cigar business. People line up for their autographs at cigar events. The adulation is well deserved. They are the only factory owners

Making cigars by hand requires
expert craftsmanship

in the industry who made the sacrifice of moving out of their comfortable home in the United States to live in difficult conditions in the country in which they make their cigars.

It is a distinct pleasure doing business with the Fuentes as one family to another. They have treated us fairly every step of the way and we have done the same in return. When we needed it, they were there for us. When they needed it, we were there for them. If I had only two dollars left to my name, I would give one of them to Carlos Fuente.

My father published a book titled *Smoke Dreams* shortly before his death in 1958. In it, he described his experiences in the cigar business and expressed his hopes for our family's continued success. In the last decade, I am proud to say, my father's smoke dreams came true beyond his wildest expectations. Undoubtedly, one of the most important factors in our continuing success is our association with the Fuente family. Another factor is a man who was a complete unknown when I first met him in 1992, but who soon became a legend in the cigar industry.

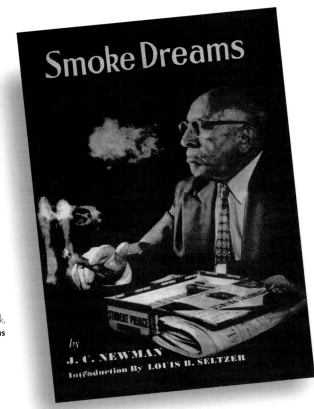

The cover of J.C. Newman's book, **Smoke Dreams**

Opposite
Top:
Carlos Fuente, Jr. explaining to M & N salesmen how tobacco is grown

Bottom:
In the tobacco fields with Carlos Fuente, Jr. and Eric

Smoke Dreams Come True

U.S. cigar consumption had been steadily declining for nearly thirty years before Marvin R. Shanken appeared on the scene. From a peak of nine billion cigars in 1964, industry sales had fallen three to five percent a year to a dismal two billion cigars in 1992. That was the year when the publisher of *Wine Spectator* first approached me about advertising in a new magazine he was planning. The magazine would be called *Cigar Aficionado*.

Marvin R. Shanken had acquired *Wine Spectator* seventeen years prior, when it was a small, relatively obscure publication. At the time, the California wine industry was on its knees; French wines had dominated the U.S. market for years. Marvin R. Shanken took this little publication and turned it into the most respected wine magazine in the world, bringing the California wine industry right along with him. By aggressively promoting and merchandizing California wines through his magazine, he helped them achieve new heights of popularity and, not incidentally, higher prices and unit sales.

He now proposed to do for cigars with *Cigar Aficionado* what he had done for California wines with *Wine Spectator*. I admit I was skeptical. I thought he might make a big splash with the first issue and then fade away. I was not alone in my opinion. The phenomenal success of *Cigar Aficionado* and the cigar boom that followed took all of us in the cigar industry by complete surprise.

The first issue was published in September 1992. Elaine and I attended the launch at the St. Regis Hotel in New York City. From the beginning, the magazine was about more than just cigars; it was about enjoying the good life. The timing was superb. *Cigar Aficionado* came out just as an American renaissance for premium products of all kinds was taking shape.

Marvin R. Shanken brought premium cigars the recognition they deserved by rating them on a hundred-point scale, making people aware of fine gradations of taste, aroma, and burning qualities. He put cigars in the same league as fine wines and other upscale products like single-malt scotches or specialty coffees. The magazine struck a chord with people, many of whom relished the idea of cigar smoking as a way of thumbing their noses at political correctness. The environment was there. All we needed was a catalyst, and Marvin R. Shanken had the vision and the chutzpah to take the ball and run with it.

He attracted an affluent subscriber base and top-class advertisers, put Hollywood celebrities and supermodels on the cover, and glorified cigar smoking as part of a glamorous lifestyle.

Top: The Newmans with General Cigar's Edgar Cullman, Jr., in front of the White House

Bottom: Bobby, me, Marvin R. Shanken, and Eric in front of the White House to support cigar smokers' rights

Eric and I share
a smoke with Arnold Schwarzenegger

Another celebrity cigar aficionado,
Jim Belushi, joins the men of M & N
and Carlos Fuente's son-in-law, Wayne Suarez

Bobby, Eric, and I light up
with Tom Selleck

CIGAR FAMILY

Elaine and I find another cigar lover
in *Miami Vice's* Michael Talbot

As it turned out, there was a pent-up demand for what *Cigar Aficionado* offered. People who had been smoking cigars for years were tired of being treated like modern-day lepers. Now they gave up their guilt and came out of the closet as proud cigar aficionados. And people who had never even thought about cigars suddenly wanted to try them. Cigars became the status symbol of the nineties.

It wasn't only the magazine, of course. Marvin R. Shanken also came up with the brilliant idea of hosting cigar extravaganzas in cities across the country. People lined up by the thousands to attend these Big Smokes, paying $150 a head for the opportunity to sample cigars. My family has attended every Big Smoke so far, sampling Cuesta-Rey and La Unica cigars. Never before had there been an opportunity like this to talk to so many of our consumers all at once. It was thrilling to witness their enthusiasm for cigars.

When cigar dinners became a popular pastime and cigar bars opened in every major city, I could only shake my head in disbelief. I can think of no other industry in American history that rebounded so vigorously from such a depressed state. And Marvin R. Shanken was at the forefront of it all: the ringmaster behind the cigar renaissance. He was a wonderful spokesman for the cigar industry. Anyone who pays half a million dollars for John F. Kennedy's humidor—as he did—knows the value of publicity. He brought the entire industry to a whole new level.

His influence has been so significant that I like to divide the cigar business into two periods: pre-Marvin and post-Marvin. And I sure like the post-Marvin period a lot better.

At the height of this miraculous cigar boom, my family celebrated our hundredth anniversary in the cigar business. We had come a long way from the first cigars my father rolled in the family barn back in 1895. To commemorate our centennial, we held a black-tie dinner at the Tampa Yacht and Country Club on September 19, 1995, attended by 185 guests including twenty-four members of the Newman family. I was particularly gratified that my brother Millard and sister Elaine accepted my invitation to celebrate with us. Fittingly, Carlos Fuente and Marvin R. Shanken were also there, and we honored them with special awards of appreciation for helping us reach this incredible milestone on such a high note.

The evening would not have been complete without some very special cigars to smoke. Nothing less than the best would do. With that in mind, I had actually begun developing an entirely new cigar five years prior to our anniversary.

I didn't care how long it took, how much it cost, or even whether it would sell or not. After almost sixty years in the business, I simply wanted to make the best cigar in the world. I had always dreamed of making an ultra-premium cigar, something of the finest quality that could be associated in the same breath with the best of the best, be it Rolex, Mercedes, or Dom Perignon.

One of the basic principles of cigar making is the thicker the cigar, the better the flavor. A thicker cigar allows for the blending of six or seven filler leaves, creating a more consistent tasting cigar. So I decided our entire line would be rolled in a fifty-four ring gauge, the thickest size on the market. My sons thought I was out of my mind.

"Have some imagination," Eric said. "Not everyone likes thick cigars. We ought to have thinner cigars in this line to appeal to more smokers."

I stuck to my guns. We developed five different lengths, all with the same thickness. It had never been done before. I approached Carlos Fuente to put aside selected bales of Connecticut Shade wrapper. After five years of fermentation, we would then open the bales and give them a second fermentation for the sweetest, richest possible taste.

I then worked with Carlos Fuente, Jr. to develop the filler blend. Carlos Jr. is just as passionate, just as smart, just as committed to excellence as his father. In my opinion, Carlos Jr.

has the finest palate for tobacco of anyone in the world; he is the best tobacco blender I have ever known. He also has the eye of an artist when it comes to packaging. He will look at a cigar label that he's developing and stare at it for five minutes without saying a word. Then he will make the most insightful comment about how to make it better, something no one else would think of. Like his father, he is an absolute perfectionist.

The Fuentes identified their most skilled cigarmakers and paid them a top, fixed rate of pay rather than by the number of cigars made—an incentive to produce the best, not the most, cigars. The Fuentes did a magnificent job making the cigars. All that remained was to come up with a name and a label. I chose the name Diamond Crown to signify what was to be our crowning achievement in premium cigars. (In fact, we had owned the brand name for over fifty years, one of the many cigar labels we had acquired but not yet used.) I then engaged the renowned Dutch lithographer Peter Vridag to produce a striking red and gold label for the cigar. Everything came together in time for our hundredth anniversary dinner and we celebrated by smoking the world's first Diamond Crown cigars.

Three generations of the Cigar Family come together to celebrate its 100th birthday

The original Diamond Crown label

A Privileged Lifestyle™

Diamond Crown today

Our supply of Diamond Crown was limited. For one thing, it takes five years to age the tobacco properly, rather than the customary two to three years. For another, the cigars are inspected three times for appearance, firmness, and texture before only fifteen out of every fifty cigars made are approved for sale. This is an exceptionally high standard compared to the usual cigar inspection process. Embarking on a national distribution for Diamond Crown right off the bat would have been impossible. Instead, we decided to introduce the cigar market-by-market, starting on the West Coast and working our way east as increased supply became available.

On April 21, 1996, we officially launched Diamond Crown in southern California with a reception in Beverly Hills at an exclusive cigar club called The Grand Havana Room. Sales exceeded our most optimistic projections. At ten to twelve dollars apiece, I was stunned to see our cigars selling out within hours of going on sale. Today, Diamond Crown sells for up to eighteen dollars apiece and we still can't make enough to meet the demand. It's a far cry from the days when raising the price of Cameo Bouquet from five to six cents destroyed half our business.

We asked tobacconists to limit the sale of Diamond Crown to two cigars per customer so that as many people as possible could try them. I heard about one customer in California who

Englebert Humperdinck comes out to celebrate the launch of Diamond Crown with Elaine and me

went to considerable lengths to circumvent the two-cigar limit. He repeatedly tried in vain to get his tobacconist to sell him a whole box. In desperation, he went home, rounded up a busload of his friends, and drove them all back to the smokeshop. He told his friends to wait in the parking lot while he went inside and asked again for a box of Diamond Crown.

"I already told you," the tobacconist said. "You can only have two cigars."

The customer opened the front door and yelled to his friends, "Okay, guys, come on in!"

As his friends piled into the store and approached the counter one by one, the customer said, "he'll take two, he'll take two, he'll take two," and so on until the retailer laughed, threw up his arms, said, "Okay, you win," and sold the man a box of Diamond Crown.

My father would never have believed it possible that someone would go to such lengths to buy cigars that sold for sixteen dollars apiece.

Perhaps my favorite Diamond Crown endorsement came from Robert Lutz, the former chairman of Chrysler. A year after we introduced Diamond Crown, I saw an interview with him in *USA Today*, which described him walking around his office with an unlit Diamond Crown. He has since said that Diamond Crown is the best non-Cuban cigar he has ever smoked. When I think that we are making the kind of cigars enjoyed by the top executives in the country, I know we've arrived.

The Diamond Crown brand proved to be a valuable asset beyond the cigar itself. Even before we put Diamond Crown cigars on the market, we introduced a line of humidors under the Diamond Crown name. In early 1995, as restaurants started participating in cigar dinners, Eric saw an opportunity. We had discontinued our Cuesta-Rey Ambassador Cabinet program in the early 1980s in response to increasing smoking restrictions in restaurants. Now seemed the perfect time to resurrect the program and put humidors filled with our cigars back in restaurants.

Eric called Reed & Barton, one of the oldest and best cabinet makers in America, and the same company that had made our Cuesta-Rey humidor cabinets back in the 1970s. It turned out that general manager Don Morrison, whom we had worked with fifteen years ago, was still with the company. He even had one of our humidors still sitting on top of his desk.

With Marvin R. Shanken

Eric discovered that Reed & Barton was also thinking about getting into the humidor business. We began to explore a possible partnership, but as Eric started to size up the situation, he had second thoughts.

"It doesn't make sense to restart this program of selling humidors with cigars to restaurants when we don't have enough cigars to take care of our smokeshops," he told me.

The cigar boom had created such a demand for premium cigars that we already had millions of cigars on back order for our existing accounts.

"Why give ourselves another distribution headache when we can't even take care of our primary customers? All we would be doing is putting out empty humidors," he said. He thought about this for a moment and then the light went on. "Well, why not sell empty humidors?"

This was in the spring of 1995 and our annual trade show for the cigar industry—the RTDA (Retail Tobacco Dealers of America)—was coming up in August. The RTDA is an invaluable venue for introducing new products; it's the best way to reach the largest number of tobacco retailers all at once. The next RTDA was only a few months away. How could we possibly develop our humidors in time?

I cautioned my sons not to rush. I feared that quality would suffer. I was especially concerned because we had decided to entrust our humidors with the Diamond Crown name. Launching Diamond Crown humidors at the 1995 RTDA meant that they would come out before the Diamond Crown cigars were available. I was concerned that if the humidors were not of the highest quality, they would damage Diamond Crown's reputation before my cigars even had a chance.

"We only get one chance at the marketplace," I said. "If we come out with an inferior product, it's all over. Let's wait until we have all our ducks in a row and come back to the marketplace when we can do it right."

Eric and Bobby didn't want to wait another year to introduce our humidors. "It's now or never," Eric said. "Who knows if the window of opportunity will still exist a year from now?"

My sons went ahead and placed an order with Reed & Barton for a thousand humidors. There was no way they would be ready in time for the RTDA, but Reed & Barton assured us they could put together five prototypes for us to display at the show.

The day before the RTDA, Eric was on pins and needles. "What if the humidors don't sell?" he kept asking. Our national sales manager, Wally Buechel, did his best to reassure him. Wally started with us when he was twenty-one years old and worked his way from the ground up. He has done his time in the trenches and has a great deal of insight into the marketplace. "They'll sell," he kept telling Eric.

He was right. We sold almost 400 humidors at the RTDA that year. It would not have happened without Mac McLaughlin, the president of the Eureka division of Reed & Barton, which makes our humidors. Mac is a terrific salesman and he gave an unbelievable sales pitch for the Diamond Crown humidors. I'm not sure he knew exactly what he was talking about—we were all new to the humidor business then—but it certainly sounded good to me. Mac inspired all of us at the RTDA that year. Without him, our humidor business would have been a flop. Instead, Diamond Crown became the best-selling line of humidors in America.

We were thrilled, especially when next year's RTDA rolled around. Everybody and his brother was selling humidors. Eric and Bobby had been absolutely right: If we had waited until then, it would have been too late for us to take the lead.

Given the success of our Diamond Crown humidors and cigars, it was only logical to extend the brand further into a full line of cigar accessories. I have always believed that we are only as good as the people we associate with, so naturally we sought out the best of the best to help us with our accessories.

When we were dissatisfied with existing cigar humidification systems, we asked Jim Pendergast, the world's foremost expert on cigar humidification, to develop a state-of-the-art humidification system for our Diamond Crown humidors. Angie Miller, whose father made Waterford crystal what it is today, worked with us to develop a line of Diamond Crown crystal ashtrays made at the renowned Miller-Rogaska crystal factory in Eastern Europe. In Spain we found one of the world's best leatherworks factories to make a line of beautiful Diamond Crown leather cigar cases.

Our overriding goal with all of these products was to provide the highest quality at the fairest price. That we have been successful in this pursuit has everything to do with the excellence of our manufacturing partners. The enthusiastic response to our accessories in the marketplace fulfilled all my hopes for establishing the Diamond Crown brand as a symbol of quality.

I have spent most of my professional life behind the scenes. As long as I could get the job done, I was content to maintain a low profile. I have been relatively well-known within the cigar industry for a long time, but I was practically unknown to the cigar smoking public until recently. When I was inducted into *Cigar Aficionado*'s Cigar Hall of Fame in March 1997, I suddenly found myself in the spotlight for the first time in my career.

It was one of the proudest moments of my life. Here I was, being honored in the esteemed company of cigar icons like Zino Davidoff, Edgar Cullman, and my good friends Carlos Fuente, Angel Oliva, and Frank Lleneza. I had been a modest player for so many years. Now I was being acknowledged as an equal among the leaders of our industry. It felt great.

A few months later, Marvin R. Shanken published a ten-page interview with me in *Cigar Aficionado*. The story came out while I was in London attending a dinner for our retailers and distributors in the United Kingdom. I was visiting a London smokeshop when several customers approached me and asked for my autograph! They had recognized me from my picture in the magazine. This had never happened to me before. I admit I enjoyed the attention of being a celebrity.

Getting attention for our family name was something my sons and I had been working on for a while, not to gratify our egos, but to strengthen our position in the marketplace. The cigar boom had caught us off guard, along with all the other established cigar manufacturers. We were unprepared for the increased demand for premium cigars, and because it takes several years to grow and age tobacco properly, it took us that long to increase our production.

This created a huge shortage of established cigar brands. Hundreds of new brands, most of them overpriced and inferior in quality, came rushing in to fill the void. Don Nobodies, we called them, since they were made by complete newcomers to the cigar industry. I actually overheard one of these rookie manufacturers boasting that he had been in the cigar business for two whole months! I had to laugh when I compared that to our 102 years of experience.

Unfortunately, consumers who had only recently started smoking cigars couldn't necessarily distinguish between superior and inferior cigars, and they bought the Don Nobodies like nobody's business. At the same time, cigar retailers had no choice but to stock these fly-by-night brands to fill empty shelf space created by the shortage. Who could blame them? In short, the Don Nobodies gained a foothold in the marketplace. Our challenge was to educate cigar smokers about the value of real experience, and communicate our longevity in the industry.

One thing was clear: Our company name wasn't helping any. The name M & N was meaningless to cigar smokers. People might see me in *Cigar Aficionado* and search in vain for a cigar made by the Newman company. At the same time, people who knew M & N might not associate it with our family. To reflect our longevity as a century-old family-owned cigar company, we decided to return to the original company name my father started with in 1895. Thus, on May 10, 1997, M & N Cigar Manufacturers was re-christened J.C. Newman Cigar Company.

My father would have been so proud. Of the 42,000 federally registered cigar companies that existed when he rolled his first cigars in the family barn in 1895, J.C. Newman Cigar Company was now the only one with a national distribution that was still owned and operated by its founding family. My father had big dreams, but even he could not have foreseen how far they would carry us.

CIGAR FAMILY

EPILOGUE
LOOKING TO THE NEXT CENTURY

When I first started working in the cigar industry, all I wanted was enough money to buy some clothes. More than six decades have passed since I earned my first paycheck in 1935 as my father's downtown Cleveland salesman, and I have come to love the whole business of manufacturing and selling cigars.

I am now 83 years old and in good health, although I had a bit of a scare back in January of 1996. I was in Miami attending a Big Smoke when my legs suddenly began to swell. Something was very wrong. I returned to Tampa to see my doctor and, after numerous examinations, was told that one of my heart valves had collapsed. Immediate surgery was recommended. As it turned out, three arteries had to be replaced, in addition to the new aorta valve.

I was in intensive care for a week following the operation. My family was by my side every single day. I have no recollection of what happened to me while I was in intensive care, but I do know this: My new heart valve came from a pig. Being of Jewish descent, this amuses me to no end. I like to tell people that my pig's valve is kosher because my rabbi, Richard Birnholz, blessed it. Funny, but true.

Six months before my heart surgery, I underwent prostate and hernia operations, so my body has certainly been well taken care of. I live a disciplined life, watch my diet, and get plenty of rest. I also exercise regularly, which keeps my pig valve from squeaking.

I'm one of the happiest men alive. I associate with the people I want to associate with and do the things I want to do. I have attained a certain position in life through hard work and a fair amount of good fortune. But I don't believe in luck. You have to make your own good luck.

I still go to the office five days a week. Over the years, I have watched too many of my contemporaries die not long after they retired. I believe the daily responsibilities of

Our 50th Wedding Anniversary

With Eric and Bobby in the Dominican Republic

Decked out for Tampa's annual Gasparilla festival

the workplace are essential to keep the mind and spirit alive. For me, retirement is not an option. I wouldn't know what to do with myself.

Like my father before me, I am always the first person to review our incoming mail every morning at the office. Unlike my father, I don't tell my sons how to respond to it. Not usually, anyway. In his latter years my father used to barge into my office, bang his fist on my desk, and exclaim: "It's time for a radical change!" I don't subject my sons to that kind of grandstanding. However, I do make my voice heard when it's time to make important decisions.

My sons are both overachievers. They have always worked long hours, although I never asked them to. It's just in their nature. They complement each other perfectly, and each has his own strengths. Eric has the ability to listen and observe, to take in ideas from different people, and then synthesize them with his own ideas into something unique that goes into the marketplace successfully. Bobby is an outstanding salesman. He has the gift of persuasion and he prepares meticulously for every sales call. Together, Eric and Bobby make an unbeatable team.

The company is in good hands under their leadership, but I would be doing them a disservice if I didn't share my ideas and observations. With more than six decades of experience in the cigar industry, I have seen it all. Sometimes I will remind them of promotions or marketing strategies that worked for us in the past, which might be valid again today. At other times, I will suggest completely new ways to differentiate us from the competition. Ninety percent of the time, the three of us are in complete agreement on the best course of action.

Of course, there is more to life than business. I have always felt a certain responsibility to my community and have devoted what time and resources I had to giving back. I have been involved with the Berkeley Preparatory School in Tampa since its founding in 1960, serving as treasurer, chairman of the building committee, and president of the Dad's Club. I have served numerous terms on the boards of the Tampa Chamber of Commerce, Saint Joseph's Hospital Foundation, our Temple, Congregation Schaarai Zedek, Tampa Rotary Club and the Latin American Fiesta, an organization promoting closer ties between the Latin and non-Latin communities. Our mayor, Dick Greco, also appointed me to serve on the Tampa Ethics Commission.

My wife is as active as I am. Elaine is the type who isn't happy unless she's completely busy. In 1978, she decided she had a little too much time on her hands and took a job as director of public relations at Maas Brothers, the leading department store in Florida. She had

With my family, being honored by the Rotary Club of Tampa

Stanford J. Newman Stadium—home of the Berkeley Buccaneers

CIGAR FAMILY

Eric in the trenches of the shipping department

Bobby enjoying his office and a cigar

Standing outside the White House with my sons and grandson, Dawson

always known how to throw a great party and here she was in her element, planning special events and parties at twenty Maas Brothers stores throughout the state. She booked quite a few celebrities for special appearances: Debbie Reynolds, Richard Simmons, Phyllis Diller, Paloma Picasso, Dr. Ruth, and lots of Miss Americas and Miss Universes. It was perfect for her.

In 1988, Robert Campeau, a wealthy financier from Montreal, purchased Maas Brothers' parent company, Allied Stores, and went on to acquire Federated Department Stores. When Campeau got into financial trouble, both companies went bankrupt. After ten years with the company, my wife's public relations position at Maas Brothers was eliminated. When they asked her to stay on in some other capacity, her response was: "I've had a wonderful time, but if I can't have a fun job, it's time for me to move on."

My eleven-year-old grandson, Drew, selling cigars at a
Retail Tobacco Dealers of America convention

Dawson dressed and destined to grow up Newman

Three generations of Newmans: Eric, Drew, and me

Elaine was just as busy as ever after she left Maas Brothers. She can't sit still. She always has at least a few balls in the air, whether it's supporting a school or fundraising for the restoration of a historic building. I hope she never slows down. Without her as my partner all these years, I wouldn't have been able to achieve what I have in this life. The fact that my sons have established happy family lives of their own brings me great joy.

Eric was introduced to his future wife, Lyris Bruce, by Robert Purvis, our chief financial officer and a trusted advisor. Eric and Lyris were married on August 12, 1978, and made a loving home together. My first grandson, Andrew Michael, whom everyone calls Drew, was born on September 3, 1981. Lyris was a schoolteacher for some time, and she has raised a remarkably intelligent and gifted son. She and Eric are both terrific parents.

My wife introduced Bobby to the woman he eventually settled down with. Sixteen weeks after he met Merideth Manee, they were engaged. On January 25, 1992, they married.

Our Tampa cigar factory today

Merideth gave birth to their first son, Charles Dawson, on May 19, 1994. On September 24, 1997, they had another son, Robert Paxton. Like Eric and Lyris, Merideth and Bobby are both loving parents.

When I grew up, my father wanted me to learn the value of a dollar. I set out to raise my sons differently. I wanted them to learn the value of a family, to help their fellow man, to be well-rounded and well-educated, and to develop strong moral character. I believe my sons have learned these lessons well. I hope that future generations of the Newman family will embrace the same philosophies with their children and continue our legacy for many years to come.

The cigar industry changes almost daily. It always has. Staying ahead of the curve is something my sons and I are very conscious of. We don't ever want to be in a situation where we're saying: "We should have done this *last* year!" Maintaining our leadership position requires tremendous flexibility. That is why we've decided to remain a private company. My advice to future executives of our company is to stay independent.

There are many benefits to remaining private. One advantage we have over our competitors is that if we want to introduce a new product or promotion, my sons and I can meet quickly and make a decision in a matter of minutes. It may be the wrong decision, but it's a decision. By the time our competitors have gone through the layers of bureaucracy required to approve a decision, the opportunity may have come and gone.

As a public company, we would also be forced to focus too much on short-term financial gains. Ever mindful of the stockholders, our competitors must constantly introduce new brands to keep up their volume. Without Wall Street looking over our shoulder, we can introduce fewer products if we choose, and focus on building brands that represent high quality and good value.

We have certainly considered going public, but we have never been willing to give up the benefits of our hands-on, long-term approach.

Our most ambitious long-term goal has been developing our international distribution. As much as I felt we had to change from a regional to a national company after World War II when people started to travel domestically, I believe it's just as important today to expand from a national to a global company now that more people are traveling internationally. In a business like ours—selling branded merchandise—global brands are essential. When people see your brand in Brussels, Paris, Sydney, Amsterdam, London, Hong Kong, and Johannesburg, it gives them confidence in the brand when they see it back home.

I have wanted to sell our cigars around the world for some time, but it was not possible until very recently. For decades the only cigars that would sell on a global basis were Cuban brands. During the last three or four years, not only was there a shortage of Cuban cigars, but the quality and reputation of Dominican cigars was greatly enhanced. This gave us the opportunity to sell our brands outside of the United States, both in Europe and the Pacific Rim. We have been quite successful in building Cuesta-Rey, La Unica, Rigoletto, and Diamond Crown internationally.

Our expansion took a great leap forward after I hired a man named John Bodycombe to head up our new international office in London. He had been with Rothmans and Dunhill for twenty-five years and was working for our importer in the United Kingdom. With his help, we have developed a tremendous business in Europe and the Middle East.

Recently, we brought Cuesta-Rey and Arturo Fuente cigars into Asia, thanks to the tireless efforts of my son, Bobby. When he first started making inroads in the Pacific Rim, almost none of our competitors were out there. In our first year in Hong Kong alone we were selling something like sixteen boxes of cigars a day, 365 days a year. We are now in more than fifty countries around the world, from Singapore to South Africa to Australia.

Looking to our next century, we must first acknowledge that the cigar boom is now over. For the most part, supply has caught up with demand and everyone is fighting for shelf space. The cigar boom was in fact a mixed blessing. The incredible demand for cigars created a tremendous deficit of product, and with millions of cigars on back order, we became more like order takers than salesmen. It is time to go back to the basics of good salesmanship. Fortunately, we know how to sell, promote, and distribute cigars as well as anyone else in the industry.

Another drawback of the cigar boom was that established brands lost market share to the Don Nobodies that glutted the market. However, the Don Nobodies have now disappeared almost completely. In the future, I believe that a few well-known brands will survive and become the quality leaders of the industry, while most new brands, whether produced by large or small cigar manufacturers, will fall by the wayside. We in our industry who market well-known brands such as Cuesta-Rey will continue to prosper and increase our market share in a greater proportion than we have in the past.

I also believe that premium cigar consumption will continue to increase for the next few years, although at a modest rate of five to ten percent rather than the double-digit growth of forty to fifty percent seen in the last three to five years.

When I first came into the business sixty years ago, consumers of tobacco products were incredibly price-conscious. Raising cigar prices by even one penny could result in the loss of fifty to seventy percent of your business. Today, the cigar market is totally different. The increased demand for premium cigars—and the higher prices manufacturers are able to charge—allow us to invest in the finest quality tobacco. As a result, premium cigars today are better than ever.

Furthermore, cigar smoking is no longer an old man's pastime. The new cigar smokers who came on board during the last several years are younger and better educated than the cigar smokers of the past. The new generation came to appreciate cigars as a high-end luxury product, a passion they can share with friends on the golf course or executives in the boardroom. A new lifestyle.

People used to smoke five to ten cigars a day. Today, because cigars are more expensive and there are fewer places where you can smoke them, people tend to smoke one a day, or perhaps only on weekends. That's fine from a manufacturer's point of view, because today's cigar smokers are willing to pay for a quality product. Most premium cigars are now priced from five to eight dollars. In the years ahead, I believe the average price will come down somewhere between four and six dollars for the majority of the business. That's still a long way from the days when most premium cigars sold for twenty-six cents.

When I was growing up, people were happy if they made enough money to pay for basic necessities—food, housing, transportation, education, and the like. Today, we live in an environment of such prosperity, with such a surplus of disposable income, that a large percentage of the population is willing to pay high prices for high quality—or what they perceive as high quality. In fact, I believe there is a greater demand for quality products than there is supply. That's a great marketplace to be in and that's why, even though the cigar industry has reached a plateau, the future of the premium cigar business looks healthy.

Celebrating the opening of the Cuesta-Rey Cigar Bar with Carlos Fuente Sr., Eric, and Larry Rothschild and Vince Naimoli of the Tampa Bay Devil Rays

With Larry Rothschild,
manager of the
Tampa Bay Devil Rays

There is a sign hanging in my office that reads:

> "If you make and sell something on the basis of
> price, someone can always make it cheaper, and
> you can be out of business in six months. But if you
> make and sell something on the basis of quality,
> you can be in business for a hundred years."

These are the words my father repeated to me again and again while I was growing up in the cigar industry. They served us well in our first hundred years in business. I believe they will continue to serve us well into our next century.

If our company is to succeed for another hundred years, there are a few more things we must keep in mind. I have shared these philosophies with my sons, and I believe they will continue to uphold them long after I'm gone.

First, if the best you can do is copy somebody else's idea, you shouldn't be in business. It's a very competitive environment. Unless you are different and innovative, nobody is going to pay attention to you. And it's not enough to think with your head. You have to bring your heart into it too. I never claimed to be the smartest man in the world, but I am passionate about what I do.

Second, try to stay well-balanced and conduct yourself with dignity. When you do get angry, try not to show it. And be forgiving. It doesn't pay to hold a grudge.

Third, treat people with fairness and respect. That goes for your employees, your customers, your suppliers—everyone you do business with. If you want to keep good people, treat them right and pay them well. Honesty, integrity, and loyalty always win out.

Here is an example of what I mean by being fair. A lot of businesses try to get their suppliers to sell to them at cost or even at a loss. I never tried to knock my suppliers down to their last penny. I would say to them: "If you can't make a profit selling to me, I don't want to do business with you."

If your vendors don't make a reasonable profit, you can be sure you won't be getting quality supplies. If I liked the tobacco a dealer showed me, I asked him the price and I paid it or I didn't. I never quibbled with anybody.

It may seem obvious, but it is also important to realize that you can only do business with someone who has money. "Poor people can only go to church together," my father often said.

The sign above our factory has become a Tampa landmark

"They can't do business together. Somebody's got to have the money. You must either buy from or sell to people who have deep pockets." That's how my father started out with so little capital. The basic principle still applies to our business today.

I can't leave out one of my strongest beliefs: the importance of brands, brands, brands. As I told Bobby when he had the opportunity to sell La Unica without labels to that retailer in Houston: "We don't sell cigars; we sell brands." It's almost impossible to build a brand, and so easy to destroy one. The leaders of our company—whoever they may be in the years ahead—would do well to remember that. If they do, they will be well on their way to a successful future.

Finally, it's vital to change with the times. I'm happy to say we have continued to innovate in response to the changing marketplace. Recently, we launched CigarFamily.com, the official Web site for J.C. Newman Cigar Company and Fuente Cigar Ltd. My grandson, Drew, was the driving force behind this, and he has helped to make it the most popular cigar site on the Internet.

We have also introduced a series of in-store cigar promotions in smokeshops across the country, offering consumers a chance to sample our cigars and win a box of Cuesta-Rey or one of our Diamond Crown accessories. These Cigar Spectaculars have done a great deal to build good will with our customers and consumers. Inevitably, our competitors have copied our idea, but that's okay.

We also introduced a company publication, the *J.C. Newman Wrapper*, which is mailed to all of our tobacconists on a quarterly basis. Retailers seem to appreciate having a regular update from us on new products, services, and policies, as well as news on the company's activities around the world.

Perhaps our most exciting new project is the Cuesta-Rey Cigar Bar, which we opened at Tropicana Field, home of the Tampa Bay Devil Rays, on March 26, 1998. It is the first cigar bar in Major League Baseball history. More than 1,000 cigar smokers come through the Cuesta-Rey Cigar Bar every night. All you have to do is walk inside to see the future of the cigar industry: The new generation of cigar smokers is there enjoying themselves.

In summary, I believe we can be in business for the next hundred years if the executives of our company remember these rules: make quality products; be innovative; stress brands; take care of your employees; treat your customers well; and be fair to your suppliers. It is also

Scenes from The Cuesta-Rey Cigar Bar:
The grand opening; patrons at the bar;
Eric presenting pitcher Wilson Alvarez of the Tampa Bay Devil
Rays with a box of Cuesta-Rey Devil Ray cigars;
With former American League home run king Frank Howard

important to be good citizens and give a percentage of your profits to charitable causes.

The cigar business was a depressed industry for most of my life. I'm glad I've been around long enough to see it transformed into a real business with a substantial future ahead. With more than a century of experience, our company is able to operate in all kinds of environments, good and bad. Sometimes it's easier to operate in adversity than it is when you're successful. It's great to be on top, but when you're up on a pedestal, people inevitably try to pull you down. We take our share of potshots from the competition, but I have every confidence that we will continue to surmount whatever obstacles lie in our path.

As we move on into our second century as a cigar family, our business is stronger than ever. La Unica is America's most popular premium cigar sold in bundles. Cuesta-Rey is one of the most popular premium Dominican cigars in the world. Diamond Crown is the best-selling humidor in the country, and one of the most coveted cigars in the industry. Even sales of our Tampa-made Rigoletto cigars are strong. And our Fuente and Newman operation is the most successful premium cigar manufacturing/distribution combination in America, and probably the world.

I would say our next century is off to a promising start.

The Newman family today (clockwise): Elaine, me, Eric, Lyris, Drew, Merideth, Dawson, Paxton, and Bobby

$\mathscr{I}$NDEX